Other Books in the Vital Worship, Healthy Congregations Series

When God Speaks through Worship:
Stories Congregations Live By
by Craig A. Satterlee

Worship Frames:
How We Shape and Interpret Our Experience of God
by Deborah J. Kapp

Leading from the Table
by Paul Galbreath

Choosing the Kingdom:
Missional Preaching for the Household of God
by John A. Dally

The Church of All Ages:
Generations Worshiping Together
Howard Vanderwell, Editor

Preaching Ethically:
Being True to the Gospel, Your Congregation, and Yourself
by Ronald D. Sisk

When God Speaks through You:
How Faith Convictions Shape Preaching and Mission
by Craig A. Satterlee

The Work of the People
by Marlea Gilbert, Christopher Grundy,
Eric T. Myers, and Stephanie Perdew

Silling the Storm
by Kathleen S. Smith

With All Thy Mind
by Robert P. Glick

When God Speaks through Change
by Craig A. Satterlee

Where 20 or 30 Are Gathered
by Peter Bush and Christine O'Reilly

Designing Worship Together
by Norma deWaal Malefyt and Howard Vanderwell

One Bread, One Body
by C. Michael Hawn

Coming Soon

From a Mustard Seed:
Enlivening Worship and Music in the Small Church
by Bruce Epperly and Daryl Hollinger

Encounters with the Holy

Encounters with the Holy

A Conversational Model for Worship Planning

Barbara Day Miller

Herndon, Virginia
www.alban.org

The Alban Institute
2121 Cooperative Way, Suite 100
Herndon, VA 20171

Cover Design by Tobias Becker, Bird Box Design.

Library of Congress Cataloging-in-Publication Data

Miller, Barbara Day, 1946-
Encounters with the Holy : a conversational model for worship planning / Barbara Day Miller.
p. cm.
Includes bibliographical references (p. 131).
ISBN 978-1-56699-398-2
1. Public worship--Planning. I. Title.
BV15.M55 2010
264--dc22

2010014277

10 11 12 13 14 VG 5 4 3 2 1

Contents

Foreword

If you are a pastor or another person in a leadership role in a local church, you have doubtless asked: "How can we deepen our common worship?" or "How can we work together to encourage this?" Barbara Day Miller sets out to answer these questions by presenting a well tested model for planning and engaging both leadership and congregation in the things that make for what Fred Pratt Green once called "a more profound Alleluia."

In retreats and seminars devoted to Christian liturgy and life, I often focus on three "heresies": when worship is done *to* the congregation, when worship is done *for* the congregation, and when there is little or very casual preparation of the assembly and the leadership for faithful participation. The first heresy is about manipulating people, especially by playing directly on emotions, or by unreflective use of sights, sounds, and symbols. The second is about worship done on behalf of a passive congregation by the "religious experts." Here the congregants become consumers. The third is about poor planning that does not attend to the pastoral and theological dimensions of faithful participation—including discernment of the assembly's capacities for worship.

This down-to-earth book sketches and opens for us a process that addresses these issues. The key is found in the quality of partnership in the leadership team—but especially in the relationships between planning, ordering the service of worship, and the qualities of leading and of pastorally informed reflection on the community's worship experience over time.

All this requires knowing the congregation and a discernment of what the assembly itself brings to what has been ordered by the leadership team. At the heart of these pages is a hope (and a blueprint) for a new kind of conversation in planning and assessing Christian public worship. Along the way this model, known here under the acronym POWR, recaptures something of the ancient practice of *mystogogy*—an intensified affective attention to what has actually been experienced in common worship. This in turn feeds the continuing cycle of planning, ordering, leading, and liturgical/theological reflection on the worship life of the local congregation.

While the book speaks well to more "free-church" orientations, it surprisingly holds strong recommendations that will be useful to both liturgical and nonliturgical traditions. The model presented here is not only practical; it awakens the possibility of a genuinely theological deepening of the meaning and point of Christian worship in relation to the life of the church in the world.

DON E. SALIERS
Wm. R. Cannon Distinguished Professor
of Theology and Worship, Emeritus
Emory University

Preface

This book outlines a process that was initiated to engage pastors-in-training in patterns of imaginative discussion and theological reflection in planning and leading worship. Worship in any setting forms us and instructs us. The practice of gathering to hear the Word, to lift praise and prayer, and to receive the feast of bread and wine makes us who we are—the body of Christ. We are also formed by the ways in which we learn to do these things. The attention to sacramental elements, the vocabulary of prayer, the protocols, and the expected gestures are all woven into the meaning of the liturgy. Careful planning for the liturgy shapes the service, which in turn shapes and forms the people who participate. Especially for pastors-in-training, the teachings we receive are likely the teachings we will practice.

At Candler School of Theology—a major denominational, ecumenical school of theology at Emory University, a large international research university where I teach and supervise worship—we were looking for a more cohesive methodology of worship planning, a better practice for teaching those who would, in turn, teach others. Before the development of the new method and structure for planning, volunteer planning teams prepared and led more than forty worship services each semester, all with different preachers or presiders at the table, and a variety of choirs and musicians. The services were often meaningful encounters with God and diverse expressions of the community's faith and practice. However, the planners had limited time together and no opportunity to consider their work after the fact. The fragmented system lacked continuity and opportunities for reflecting on either the planning or the worship services.

We initially conceived this model as a practical guide to enrich the liturgical life of our community and better equip our students for ministry. We set out to be more efficient in preparing for worship, more pedagogically sound and effective in leadership training. And this did happen; we did reach our goals. The worship services are more cohesive and flow more smoothly. Our worship life has become richer—more thoughtful, more joyous, more inclusive and welcoming. Volunteer leadership has become confident and competent, attendance has increased, and more volunteers have signed up for leadership roles.

As we reflected on the process, it became apparent that these positive changes were not just a product of our planning and carefully articulated goals. The enriched teaching, leading, and worshiping were consequences of the conversations themselves. The deep relationships and the practice of listening, reflecting, sharing ideas, and caring for one another over time were added gifts. We discovered that while the questions in each step were important for guiding our thoughts and discussions, paying attention to the personal interaction was more essential. We brought the fruits of this spiritual engagement into worship in the presence of God and God's people. In making space for hearing other voices and other perspectives, we had made space for the work of God's Spirit among the members of the seminary community.

With a covenant for presence, conversational engagement, and mutual respect, the members of the various planning teams now meet for one hour each week throughout the semester to plan and prepare worship services as assigned. In creative and thoughtful discussion, members learn to articulate their own denominational, cultural, and regional practices; they learn to speak across differences and listen to those unlike themselves. They learn to use a variety of resources and to work with the preacher of the day to shape and facilitate the time of worship. After the worship service, they reflect on what happened in that sacred time and begin the process again.

Asked about the process and its effect on their own vocations and spiritual lives, students spoke of deepened self-awareness, gratitude for the study of scriptural texts and liturgical resources, an appreciation for challenging and creative conversation, and profound thanks for new friendships and shared experience. Most of all, they testified to a more informed participation in worship and a life more fully lived in the presence of God.

In the second phase of development, we introduced the planning model into selected congregations to see whether the concepts and patterns would enrich worship life in these parishes. We joined with twenty local churches of various sizes—from small rural congregations to those in county-seat towns to "big-steeple" churches. We launched the model in a new church start where most members had no church background, and in an urban church with longstanding lay leadership. Worship styles varied from contemporary to "high church" and included midweek gatherings sponsored by campus ministries.

The pastors and members of those worshiping communities are the conversation partners of this book. They tell their own stories of renewed worship, of deepened faith, of more enlivened praise of God. They also tell of difficulties, pastoral longings and discernment, and the evolutions of the planning process. They, like you, are men and women serving God's people in congregations around the country. Perhaps you can picture yourselves among them; perhaps you will hear your own voice in these pages. Because this is a conversation, the pattern is continually evolving; questions lead to more questions. Because the conversation brings together a wide range of interested and curious and faithful people, we will be surprised by the lively presence of the Spirit.

Welcome to the holy work of planning, ordering, leading, and reflecting on the worship life where you are. You are in good company. Invite others to join you as we begin this discussion.

Acknowledgments

In this book centered on conversation, I am indebted to many who have been engaged in discussions and dialogue about worship. Their insights, good advice, questions, and notes have been critical contributions for which I am grateful. I am remembering them all, and mentioning some by name:

Gail O'Day, senior associate dean of faculty at Candler School of Theology, who first nudged me to apply for a grant from the Calvin Institute for Christian Worship. Two grants from CICW have supported the development of the POWR planning model.

Betty Grit, renewal grants coordinator at CICW, gentle guide and a strong and joyful woman. Our ongoing conversations with her and others at Calvin, face to face and in e-mails and reports, have kept us on track, helped us shape the questions, and affirmed our progress.

Yvi, Meredith, Keith, Jonathan, Stephanie, Ed, Toni, Beth, Sara, and Rebecca, student staff in the Office of Worship at Candler whose passion for worship, insistence on excellence, and intentionality in planning and leading worship helped birth this conversational model. Now serving in local parishes, they continue to question, critique, imagine, recruit, train, rehearse, lead, welcome, write, and pray so that the sacred space and the gathered people might be prepared for the in-breaking of the Spirit of God. They are an inspiration to me and a great gift to the church.

Scott, Mollie, Matt, Matt, Jenny, Marsha, Katye, Lisa, John, Jae, Keith, Beth, Tommy, Thomas, Jason, Jonathan, Stephanie, and Nate, pastors of the parishes who worked out the kinks in the POWR model and who came to Candler for consultations. You can see and hear yourselves in these pages. Hopefully, the quotes are correct!

Kevin, Mike, Jeff, Christina, Jan, and Randall, student pastors in my worship planning classes, who drive to and from seminary in Atlanta every week so that small parishes in Mississippi, Alabama, South Carolina, and Georgia might be led in the praise of God. Your leadership and skill enable the interconnected body of Christ to gather, to listen, to respond and remember, and to be empowered for God's work in the world.

Beth Gaede, editor, long-distance friend. With margin notes and questions in bold type, she is probing and exacting, seeking clarity and precision, and generally cleaning up excessive verbiage. (Even now she might say, "Need all those words?"). So, I put it simply: "Thank you, Beth!"

Carlton "Sam" Young, my teacher and valued friend for more than thirty years. His expansive knowledge, prophetic insights, and deep wisdom inspire me, and his encouraging words are a great gift.

Chapter 1

Worship and the People

Gathered in God's Presence

The sound of the tower bell echoes across the parking lot and into the streets beyond. As it has for many years, the chiming of the hour calls the community to worship. People come from every direction. Some walk from nearby apartments; some have driven from a distance; some come in the van from the retirement home; two have spent the night in a homeless shelter down the street. They come alone, with friends, with family. The doors of First Church open onto the street, welcoming the neighborhood. As they enter, the people are embraced by the sound of the hymn "God, you call us to this place . . ."[1]

On the Sabbath the people who gather in Christ's name want to participate in excellent worship. They want to offer their best to God, and they want to be led in ways that encourage that offering. They want to feast at a table that joins them to people of other places and times. They want to learn and participate in a language of prayer that connects them with God, one another, and the world. They desire worship that brings them into the heart of God. As Tom Long, well-known professor of preaching, has recently written, "People are not hungry for more worship services, for more hymns, sermons, and anthems. They are hungry for experiences of God, which can come through worship; in the most primal sense, this hunger is what beckons people to worship. The anticipation of the holy is almost palpable, even in the tiniest church on the most routine of days."[2]

However, as Long says, people do not need more of the same. Nor will they necessarily be satisfied by a shift in the order of worship or a completely new repertoire of songs. Worship must nourish a range of hungers—the hunger for a word of forgiveness and a sign of hope, the thirst for the Good News of new life. This is a complex hunger, and the work of worship itself is complex and multidimensional.

Dimensions of Worship

As we prepare to introduce a new model for planning worship, let's begin with a closer look at the ways all the elements of the worship service work together to bring worshipers into the presence of God and thereby form them in faith. Examining the many facets of worship involves more than analyzing or measuring the congregation's participation in the rituals of the service. Indeed, this close look involves attention to the totality of what professor of Christian education Jane Rogers Vann calls the "dimensions of worship." In her book *Gathered Before God*, Vann asserts that worship is "experienced simultaneously on many levels of human receptivity and understanding."[3] In other words, we worship with mind and heart, body and soul. The dimensions of worship—physical/sensory, affective, narrative, cognitive, social/relational and imaginative—are subtle aspects and effects. They are a way of talking about and defining a multifaceted and multisensory encounter with God.

Worship of God in the assembly of the faithful is an embodied activity. Liturgical theologian and professor Don Saliers has often said that worship is "touching and speaking and celebrating in God's name."[4] The physicality of worship encompasses all our senses; it is the whole self enacting our praise. We hear the bells calling us to gather, the voices singing beloved hymns, the words of grace and challenge, the sound of our own names as we remember baptismal vows. We hear the stories—the narratives of Scripture and the echoes of our living memories in this place. We see the sun through the stained-glass windows; we see the faces of those we know, those we have yet to know, and those saints who have passed on yet still surround us. We observe ancient symbols of the faith and signs of new technology. We smell the bread, the lilies, the Chrismon tree, the mustiness of the hymnals in the racks, the polish on the wood. We feel the embrace of welcome, the water in the font, the weight of the worn Bible in our hands, the ashes on our forehead. We taste the bread and wine. We move as we are able, to stand, to kneel, to bring candidates to the font, to receive bread with outstretched hands, to dance, play instruments, wave banners, and offer gifts of self and resources. In all these actions, the senses are engaged and sharpened; our worship is multisensory. We embody the praise of God.

The movement and the sensory experiences shape us in the patterns of worship and form us in faith. Just ask any older member of the congregation. Julia may not recall the most recent sermon, but when she sings "Jesus, Keep Me Near the Cross," she can vividly recall sitting in the pew next to her mother and the smell of their wool coats in winter. The memory itself is a reminder of the whole of her identity. Or consider the youngest children. Jack is just beginning to participate in the worship life of the community. At age three, he is not singing the songs or comprehending the words of the sermon or the long prayers. He does, however, eagerly await "my blessing" when, at the communion, he kneels at the altar rail, folds his hands, looks up with wide eyes, and feels the hand of the priest on his head as she says, "Jack, always remember that God loves you." As we worship God, we are formed in this disposition of praise; we come to know who we are; we become what we do.

In worship we are stretched to acknowledge before God all that we are. The spiritual affections are the deepest longings of the human heart—the inexpressible joy as well as the overwhelming sorrow, awe, and wonder in the presence of God, and the tender feelings of "coming home." We search for a heart-language with which we can relate the truth about ourselves to God. We learn this language in the emotional range of the psalms, in the rich metaphors of the hymns of our faith, and in sermons and prayers that embrace the fullness of human experience and the totality of human affection.

We sing, "I love to tell the story of Jesus and his love." We are people of that story. The Christian story is living, incarnate; it has flesh. We enact the narrative of our faith in pageant, drama, song, and dance. We enter into the story as the Word is read and proclaimed, brought to life in our assembly, and as we weave that story with our own family stories, coming into the presence of the saints. We become a part of the story as we celebrate: "pour out Your Spirit upon us and on these gifts . . . take and eat."[5] We are the story in the world as we engage in acts of compassion and justice.

We are the living body of Christ—broken, shared, and sharing. We care for one another in the various times and circumstances of our lives. A Sunday school class that began as the "young couples' class" continues to nurture the same members into their final years. We know the comfort of our accustomed seats in the congregation. We notice who is missing. We observe the greetings of members and visitors. We engage with multiple generations; we assist one another, learn from one another. We also remind ourselves of those who are not present—those who might not be welcomed, those in need, in pain. We note who is given particular recognition; which people are in charge; which people become invisible. Where are the children? The infirm? The aged?

We gather at the table for the feast that proclaims an eschatological hope: "until Christ comes in final victory and we feast at the heavenly banquet."[6] Our own living and dying give witness to this faith and the promise of God fulfilled. "In life, in death, in life beyond death, God is with us. We are not alone. Thanks be to God."[7]

Knowing the Congregation

These are the deep encounters with God and one another for which we hunger as we gather for worship. The primary work of the pastor is to lead worship services that can feed this hunger. If you are the pastor, you know this call to holy work. You have been formed in this very identity and given authority by the church to preach the gospel, to preside over sacramental celebrations, and to order the worship life of the church. Now you are prayerfully seeking new ways to lead the congregation into worship that will empower the worshipers for ministry in the world.

In reflecting on the interwoven dimensions of worship in your congregation, you are beginning to prepare for the expanded model of planning that this book outlines. This model will call you to be aware of all the sensory elements in worship—seeing and hearing, but also tasting and smelling and touching. You will give attention to the ways people learn the stories of faith, express their deep affections, and enact their care of one another. You will come to know more fully those who worship in your church. Who are the people who sit beside one another each week, who greet one another warmly and welcome the stranger with a cup of coffee? What is their relationship to one another, to the community? How are they being formed by worship and sent to be the church in the world?

As you introduce a new model for planning the liturgy, the work of all the people, you need to know more about the very people who gather for this work. I recommend a survey or a series of small-group conversations about the worship life of the congregation. These are also ways to introduce a language of the Spirit, a theological language that can assist members in speaking about their worship of God. Through the conversations or the survey you will discover some of the spiritual longings of the congregation. The people's responses will give you insights into the ways they are being formed into the likeness of Christ through the liturgical practices in which they have been and are engaged.

Appendix A is a sample survey for use in your congregation, either with written responses or conversation in small groups. You might also put these open-ended statements on large charts located in the fellowship space and invite people to jot down their names and responses—a few words, a drawing, a question—as they share coffee and conversation. Unlike surveys with quantifiable questions, the open-ended phrases in this survey are not weighted in any direction. People may respond to some or all of the sentence-starters in any way they choose. At Candler "the Eucharist" was often named as one of the most meaningful parts of our worship life together. The phrases encouraged people to articulate that perception more fully. When we celebrate Holy Communion, I "look at all those around the table together," "am made aware of the community that forgives," "appreciate 'receiving' the bread," "recite the prayer with the presider and partake of the remembrance of Christ's sacrifice," "am rejuvenated," "remember the grace of God poured out for *me*." The survey provides space for a multiplicity of responses; there are no correct answers.

Articulating a Vision

Having listened to the conversations and compiled the survey answers, you will begin to understand which elements of the worship celebration are nourishing to the people and which of their hungers are not being fed. You may be surprised by the diversity of tastes and opinions as you begin to categorize responses to the survey topics—the most engaging elements of worship, the list of meaningful songs, the responses to hearing the Word preached or to celebrating Holy Communion. You will note the depth of needs reflected in the questions ("I've always wanted to ask. . .") and the longings ("Our worship would be more engaging/inviting if. . ."). You will discover that along with the celebrations, many opportunities for learning and growing together emerge as you plan and prepare for worship.

Listen prayerfully to the longings of your own heart; listen to the echoes of the people's conversations. Engage the music director and other key leaders or staff members in conversation. Discern together the spiritual and liturgical needs of your congregation and the specific ways that careful worship planning can facilitate renewal. What do you desire from worship for the people you serve? If the new planning model was effective, how would that change the worship life of the congregation? How would planning enhance the liturgy? How would your own ministry be strengthened? The paragraphs below reflect conversations from other pastors and churches. Their findings may help focus your own list of expectations.

Deeper formation: One pastor said, "I hope that this involvement in the ongoing work of preparing for worship will educate members of our congregation, so that their own experience of liturgical celebration will be expanded and deepened; that they would have a deeper knowledge of the Scripture, of our heritage of liturgical practice, more enthusiasm for the worship service—an expectation that God does and will meet us here." You may be aware of this need in your own congregation and long for teaching opportunities *about* worship as you work to plan *for* worship so that the people of all ages can be more fully formed in faith.

Expanded practice: The survey and conversations may reveal the desire to celebrate the Eucharist more frequently or to sing a wider range of congregational songs and service music. How can the liturgy include varied musical styles or prayer language? You may have been surprised to note how many of the familiar favorite "songs of the heart" have—or have not—been sung recently in worship. Or that a member's list of favorites includes a wide range of styles: "How Firm a Foundation," "Santo, Santo, Santo," and "Shout to the Lord."

Increased lay leadership: You may realize that many whose voices were heard in the survey have not been asked to assist in various liturgical roles—readers, servers, greeters, etc. As a result, you might ask: How are volunteers being recruited? How could we expand and improve the training for these ministries? Another pastor commented: "Since liturgy is the work of the people, it is my hope that much of the behind-the-scenes work would be 'farmed out' so that more and more people would have a share in the preservice offerings that make the celebration happen."

Refreshment and renewal: In describing their experience of worship, some people may have said, "routine." You may feel that way yourself. While you continue to celebrate the "most engaging acts," what might renew worship life? How would dramatic presentations of the texts and biblical story refresh our spirits and engage our minds? How can we find language to express the full range of our affections in prayer?

Hospitality and mission: A pastor reflected: "I want our worship life to remind us of those just outside the doors, the neighbors we need to welcome. I want our worship to strengthen us for service and ministry in the world." How might worship form the people into a community of hospitality? How can the congregation learn to make space for and appreciate the voice and presence of the other?

> In response to "A question I have . . . ," one person wrote, "What is that smoking gold ball?" The simple answer is, "a thurible" [or incense burner]. But we sensed the question was really asking for more information about the details of our liturgical practices and why they are important. So we advertised a one-hour session called "The Smoking Gold Ball and Other Liturgical Mysteries Revealed." It was a lighthearted, informative introduction of a whole new language for many. We set out the altarware: paten, chalice, purificator, corporal; we modeled vestments: chasuble, cassock, cotta, cincture, stoles. And, of course, the smoking gold ball! We explained the historic origins of each item and its significance in the liturgy. Questions were flying: "What is. . . ?" "How do you use. . . ?" "Why. . . ???" Through the explanations, the mysteries were revealed. And by being informed, the people were prepared to participate in the deeper mysteries to which these "things" pointed.
>
> —Office of Worship, Candler School of Theology

The conversation has begun. The people in the congregation are thinking and talking about worship. Their responses to the survey and engagement in guided conversation are making them more conscious of the ways they participate in worship. The musicians and other staff have begun imagining: "What if we . . . ?" The pastor is listening to this discussion—some points predictable and others surprising. She may be overwhelmed by the hungers, the needs, the questions. She may also be affirmed by the evident spiritual depth in the congregation. Everyone is ready to get started, to join in an expanded conversation about planning and preparing for worship, for the people's work in the liturgy. The next chapter outlines the process.

Chapter 2

Formed by the Practices

Introducing the Planning Model

Lisa was chair of the worship committee in a large suburban church. She sang in the choir. She had grown up in this denomination and knew its liturgy well. She was also experienced in leading committees and vision task forces. She knew how to outline agendas and devise strategies. But in the monthly meetings of the worship committee, she just could not move the conversation beyond reports of what had recently occurred in worship and less-than-energetic planning for upcoming services. She had expressed her frustration to the pastor. Was it her leadership? Were the committee members not interested in real planning or new ideas for worship? How could they find a more effective path for planning worship?

Worship planning, whether it's led by a pastor, a musician, a planning team, or a worship committee, begins with this goal in mind: a well-thought-out liturgy that involves the assembly in authentic praise of God. In most congregations, regardless of the church's size or style of worship, elements of the service—music, prayer, sermon, movement to the table and out into the world—are placed in an established order that will guide the congregation in the worship hour. After the service, any reflection is usually an evaluation of particular elements of worship—this went well; this did not. The pattern is repeated weekly and seasonally.

Often the planners (clergy, musicians, lay members of various functional committees—altar guild, ushers, technicians) anticipate the whole of the service through their own roles in worship. Each sees worship through a particular lens. Musicians are concerned mainly with the anthem or the hymns and songs; ushers focus on the efficiency of seating guests or the smoothness of collecting offerings. The planning revolves around predictable choices and sequences, putting elements of the worship service into established places, into their proper "slots." For example, no matter its style or theme, the choral anthem is always sung at the offertory. The language of any postservice reflection is functional and generally focuses on practical improvements. "Last week we ran out of bulletins, so let's remember to print more." "The choir needs to begin the procession on the first stanza."

This common method of planning and reflecting is basically linear. It is a logical method of preparing the service because the worship service itself (the liturgical *ordo*) is a sequential pattern. With contextual and denominational variations, the established pattern—gathering, hearing, responding, departing—sustains the congregation in the rhythms of praise and prayer. The shape of the service is dependable and familiar. The assembly is formed in and by the flow and sequence of the liturgy.

While this common pattern of planning is functional, a more expansive and spacious liturgical celebration calls for preparatory conversation that is fluid. For the worship to be multidimensional and multisensory, the planning itself has to expand to include language that is poetic and playful as well as declarative or practical. Brainstorming and imagining offer an open way of thinking and discussing that is more circular than linear. Brainstorming has no expectations of "right answers," but will elicit ideas that can seem completely unrelated to one another. A circular discussion, by definition, does not move in one direction.

While creative and exciting, an exclusively circular planning conversation can spin on and on, with great ideas but no focus, no defining order. Conversely, a solely linear process can become a series of lists, with limited opportunity for change or expansion. Linear and circular thinking are distinct, but both are useful and must be held in tension as necessary components of planning.

The challenge is to plan multisensory worship services that are structured and focused. The task requires imaginative conversation about the biblical text as well as practical preparation. The worship service requires order and flow that incorporate the assembly's expressions of joy and awe and thanks and lament. As we developed the conversational model, we learned that separating the two movements of "planning" and "ordering" was the key to working with this tension. In our conception, the planning is more free-form; it involves discovery of multiple possibilities and expressions based on the biblical texts. Ordering is more linear, more sequential; this step puts the pieces in place.

Distinguishing the imaginative/affective conversation from the functional/equipping process allows for diverse ideas and interpretations as well as for careful organization. The discussion among members of the planning team is more spacious; there is no rush to put the ideas into "slots." In ordering the service, planners base their outlining of the logistics on the needs of the worship service, as well as on local custom.

As we gained skill in practicing this conversation, moving from *planning* to *ordering*, then into *worship* and the *reflection* that followed, we adopted an acronym for the conversational process: POWR (pronounced "power"). The POWR model goes beyond merely preparing worship services. It includes the work of preparing the people who will worship—through study and discussion, questioning and wondering—so that they might worship more honestly and live more faithfully. This process guides the planners and leaders and congregants, uniting a community of diverse spiritual practices and expressions into a vibrant, worshiping congregation through word and gesture, song and prayer, preaching and sacrament.

Foundational Principles

The underlying premise of the POWR model is that planning and preparing for worship is holy work. We study Scripture, prepare and order the service, and train leaders not *in order* to worship. The planning and preparation are themselves opportunities to experience the Holy, to see God's Spirit at work in us. Through attentive conversation, training, and rehearsal, we become more informed and better prepared leaders and worshipers, better able to listen, participate, and reflect. We learn to live into our call to be the body of Christ. We are formed by practice.

Word

In this practice of planning and preparing for worship, we are led by the Word of God. The texts for the day and the season are the starting point. Whether the pastor preaches a sermon series based on a selection of texts or follows the lectionary, the biblical texts drive the planning. The Revised Common Lectionary is the suggested three-year cycle of assigned readings for Sundays and feast days. This guide, held in common by multiple denominations, leads us through the Christian year and the liturgical life that teaches us and shapes us as disciples of Jesus, following in his way. An unfolding pattern of Scripture holds preachers and musicians and planners accountable to the Word. The lectionary provides opportunity for seasonal as well as weekly planning, and for preaching series using the suggested texts. We do not need to look for a text; the Word comes to us. As the planning team studies the texts and orders the components of the service, the team and the congregation are continuously involved in the Word. Through hymns and songs and prayers that echo the biblical texts, the people of God are shaped by and participate in the story.

Sacraments

The conversational model takes seriously the sacramental life of the church. Our entry into the life of Christ through baptism and our continued feasting in the weekly Eucharist, or Holy Communion, are the primary means of grace. These actions are the people's response to the Word. Those planning the liturgy provide for the congregation's full participation in multisensory and multidimensional celebrations of God's generous gifts of water and bread and wine. The planners and pastor make certain that worshipers can see and hear the water poured, that all receive real food at the table. Planners give attention to training servers, acolytes, ushers, and other lay volunteers, who then serve with confidence, embodying the ministry of all Christians. Because the people and leaders are prepared, the pastor can focus on priestly leadership at the table and font.

Ecumenicity

Though acting locally, we are a part of the worldwide church, and so our planning embraces an ecumenical and global understanding of Christian liturgy. In a practical sense, this awareness prompts us to use a wide range of musical and textual resources developed by poets and composers from many times and places. The worshipers in one congregation learn to sing and to join in the songs of Christians in other locations—across town or across the world. When we include global songs and rhythms, when we read Scripture in other languages, we provide hospitality to the stranger and a welcome to the neighbor. In addition, this ecumenical orientation calls us to articulate more clearly our own faith community's theology and practice—why we do this and what that means for the world.

You will discover that, more than providing a systematic process or structured outline to follow or a set of steps toward worship renewal, the POWR model offers a flexible, guided pattern of conversation among the people of God in a congregation. Though simple in its outline, the process itself is not always easy. Striving for simplicity is often more difficult than elaboration. It is, however, deeply rewarding, exciting and life-giving. Chapter 3 suggests options for organizing the planning teams to fit your own context.

Our youth minister began bringing the youth together weekly to talk about their Sunday-night service, brainstorming ideas and coordinating song sets to coincide with the message for each week. The results have been astounding. Not only do the youth have a say in the planning, but they are developing leadership roles and understanding more and more about worship. (Pretty amazing when you think that our oldest team member is a tenth grader!) Their biggest struggle is the reflection time after the service. Mostly the focus is on "That was cool!" but a more precise articulation will come in time.

—Jonathan, Associate Pastor

Planning

The first step in planning is listening to and "seeing" the biblical texts, reimagining the scriptural themes in concrete expression. In this session, the fundamental question is "What is God saying to us in the Word for this day?" This is a time of prayerful reading of the text or texts, after which the leader, usually the pastor, invites responses. The questions guide the conversation toward affective and internal reactions to the reading. In the brainstorming that follows, quick reflections, one-word descriptors of the themes of the text, and probing questions all fill the air and bounce against one another. No idea is judged or eliminated; all are given space. As the process continues, the planners consider the congregation and the season of the church year. Particular questions guide the discussion: How are we giving expression to this liturgical season—with color or music or gesture? How do the themes of the biblical text speak to our own congregation? What languages shall we use to express our response? Which hymns or prayers or movements? Shall we speak or sing or dance the psalm? Planners are encouraged to articulate a multiplicity of choices. This initial gathering of the team ends with a bundle of notes and suggestions. Some thoughts may still be swirling as the group dismisses.

> While few, if any, of our laypeople were capable of brainstorming specifics, they were all capable of having an experience of the Scripture. So, that's where I started. I read the Scripture for the day, and I asked questions to elicit the emotional response to those readings. For whatever reason, they *loved* doing this. It opened up discussion of how the narrative of the text worked, the effect of the images, the reasoning behind it, etc.
>
> —NATE, PASTOR OF A NEWLY ORGANIZED CONGREGATION

Ordering

The ordering session involves untying the bundle of ideas from the planning time and arranging them within the liturgical structure. As noted earlier, a basic structure is in place, whether as a historic, fourfold *ordo* or "the way we worship here." The "central things," as liturgical theologian Gordon Lathrop says—the font and the table, our identity and our food, the gathering and hearing, the thanksgiving and departing—are the patterns in which the people are already formed or are being formed. In the time between "planning" and "ordering," some of the ideas will have wilted, some will have disappeared, and others will have come into full bloom. ("It's clear we need to begin with this hymn." "Then the dancers could bring in the elements for the communion.") The conversation revolves around the purpose of and need for various elements in the liturgy and the practices of the parish. The pastor or planning-team leader has opportunity for catechesis, for teaching the history and meaning of the gestures and language of worship. The planners consider the practical aspects of the service and the leadership needed for the praise of God on this day. Their work involves lists and training and rehearsal; they are concerned with the preparation of space and elements. Always, the underlying question is "How can we respond to God's Word in ways that are truthful, ways that call, nourish, and send us to be the church in the world?"

After a while, as we put the service in order, the planners had more questions about the "how" and "why" of our worship: How does the lectionary organize the season? How do the lectionary Scriptures, taken in seasonal chunks, suggest ways to visually adorn the space as well as guide spiritual disciplines? Why do we use the eucharistic prayers that are set forth in the book of worship? Why are we committed to the structure of the prayer itself? How is the weekly eucharistic celebration connected to the Scripture of the season?

—Matt, pastor of an urban congregation

Worshiping

In worship, the people of God gather for praise and prayer, confession and celebration. They expect a Word from the Lord. The circular and imaginative conversation of planning and the linear and functional organizing all come together in the poetry of hymns, the giving and receiving of the offering, the expected gesture of sharing bread, and the unexpected sunlight shining through the window on the heads of children at the altar. People who are drawn to varied expressions of worship find a welcome place. Their songs are heard, their prayers given voice. Those who have planned and studied and suggested ideas and those who have trained the servers and acolytes and choir see this preparatory work offered to God. The multifaceted planning and ordering come to full expression in the gathered assembly's worship.

Reflecting

The holy work of the planning team continues after worship. The team comes together to pray and to reflect on what happened in the community's gathering before God. Deeper and more constructive than a list of what was "good" or "not good" about the service, the conversation is about God's actions, God's presence in worship. In the first part of this session, participants recall images and feelings. "What words describe the worship service?" "In what ways was God revealed in this time?" "What were the sensory experiences—tasting, touching, hearing, seeing—through which we encountered the risen Christ?" Then the conversation moves to logistical and functional questions about space and preparation, and practical elements like lighting and sound. The conversation begins with God's actions, God's presence. Subsequently, the conversation involves more practical aspects.

Through this reflection, the pastor and the planning team members are once again brought around to the beginning of the process. "What is God saying to us this day, and how might we respond?"

> We reflected on the ways in which God was working in us and through us. We noted the increased participation in the ritual actions—singing, praying the petitions, gestures to and with the presider, singing the communion, and a greater sense of purpose about the Eucharist and a greater appreciation of its central role in worship.
>
> —MATT, PASTOR OF AN URBAN CONGREGATION

Summary

Rather than helping to structure a series of worship services punctuated by preparatory meetings, the conversational model involves discussion that is both imaginative and functional. The planning team gives explicit attention to fleshing out the liturgy, making visible God's invitation and our response through specific actions and gestures, signs and symbols in *this* place. We trust that the same Spirit that is at work in and through us in our common work, the liturgy, also enlivens our conversation and preparation.

Over time, through careful planning, ordering, and reflecting, worship becomes richer, not routine or habitual. Rituals are more meaningful and well led; gestures are practiced and solid; the service has a cohesive flow. The pastor is energized, and the people are empowered for their work of worship. The pastor, musicians, planners, and the whole congregation enjoy a deeper spiritual life. The planning group becomes a covenant circle of accountability. Team members learn to speak clearly and listen well. In return, each is affirmed and welcomed in his or her uniqueness. It is a grace-filled pattern that weaves together the preparation for and the response to worship. The rhythms of circular and linear thinking that engage both mind and heart lead to an ongoing encounter with the Holy.

Chapter 3

The Planning Team

Inviting the Conversation Partners

Jeff was flattered, excited, and a little hesitant when Pastor Margaret invited him to be a part of a new worship planning team. A longtime member of the church, he had been involved in various ministries and knew most of the congregation by name. Although Jeff had never served on the worship committee, he led an usher team and had observed that worship had become more predictable over the past few years. That wasn't a negative thing; worship wasn't boring or lifeless, but he longed for a deeper experience of God in worship. Conversations with other ushers and Sunday school class members had revealed similar perceptions among his friends. So when Pastor Margaret said they would be studying the lectionary texts together and seeking to give new expression to the message through music, drama, visuals, and sound, Jeff was interested. Because he was ready for a new experience and trusted Margaret and her leadership, Jeff agreed to be a part of the conversation.

Who are the planning conversation partners in your congregation? Who should be included on the planning team? How can you form a group whose members are accountable to one another and caring of the whole congregation? What, exactly, are these people called to do?

Membership on the Planning Team

The pastor and the music leader (whether minister of music, praise-team leader, or volunteer pianist) have central roles on the planning team and are included in the conversations, whether present in every meeting or closely consulted as the work unfolds. They will need to confer as the pastor considers who might be members of the planning team.

If you are the pastor, you have probably thought of other people who should participate in the discussions, who will contribute ideas and listen well, and who have an interest in worship. You will want to invite some seasoned worship planners as you introduce this new model—people who may have "never done it this way before" but nevertheless will embrace new ideas and welcome surprises. You will want to include those who know the history of your parish, who are acquainted with the congregation's unique characteristics, and who know the traditions of your church. And you should invite new members—those who may tell you they know nothing about planning worship, but who will readily explore ideas and ask questions. In your prayerful search, look for those who are curious—who are open and excited and who want to know and experience the whole of the Christian story.

Reread the survey results (from the example in chapter 1). Who completed the survey? How are the survey participants connected with the worship life of the congregation? How do they participate in worship? What parts of the service speak to them in the most profound ways? Look at the variety of responses—from those who are "at home" and those who "wish we could. . ." Some people may have listed favorite hymns that are new to this congregation. Others may hope to celebrate Holy Communion every week, or to participate in an intense study of the upcoming preaching texts. How can these people and their ideas be included in the worship planning? What do people wonder about? What do they long for? Who is inquisitive, confident, quiet? Pray for all who responded to the survey questions. You will invite some of them to do the work of planning worship.

Extending the Invitation

When you invite parish members into this conversation, they will have some practical questions about time commitments and preparations. You will need to articulate clearly what is expected.

1. *The commitment of time.* Where, when, and how long is each of the team meetings? What is the members' expected length of service? One year? One season? One particular event?
2. *Support for this ministry.* What resources will the team have? What print or electronic sources for music, prayers, and visual designs will be available? Is there money set aside for purchase of fabric or altar furnishings?
3. *Leadership and guidance.* Who will lead the team into this new pattern? How will the team be prepared and trained for the work?

The following options are suggestions for structuring the team and preparing the planners.

Structuring the Team and Its Work

The ministry of planning can be structured in any of several ways. There is no one correct way to organize the groups because there is no single way to be the church. The examples that follow are from our pastor colleagues and the congregations in which we introduced the planning model. These structures and the schedules for completing the work have evolved and expanded as the volunteers became more familiar with the process and as the laity assumed more leadership. You may see a model that will work for your congregation, or you may choose to modify or combine several options.

The Congregation Is the Team

In one small rural church, the worship planning discussion grew out of after-church conversations. John, the pastor, reports:

> In the first six months of my appointment, I *was* the planning team. Worship was up to me. I planned; I led. I was looking for new ways to encourage the people, to get them involved, to help them see that this was their church. We began meeting informally for a few minutes after church to reflect on the service. Then,

> after a while, we decided to meet over lunch and talk about the upcoming Sundays. Using the pattern of planning and ordering, the people themselves became the team.

This organic creation of a team works well in a very small congregation. The weekly lunchtime meeting was the norm for about three months until the team and the process were established. Now John reports using a model that is less time-consuming:

*****

PLANNING TEAM: Six to eight regular worshipers, including pastor and pianist.

SCOPE OF RESPONSIBILITY: The team plans and orders all the worship services. The pastor advises and has final approval.

LENGTH OF SERVICE: In this small congregation, members rotate on and off in a rather informal way, generally serving from six months to a year.

SCHEDULE:

Planning: One meeting per month after worship with a meal together. Plan several weeks ahead in one session.

Ordering: Mostly by e-mail and brief meetings after worship.

Reflecting: Conversation with the congregation after the service; more extended discussion at the beginning of the weekly adult Sunday-school class meeting.

*****

The Worship Leaders Become the Team

Jonathan is the associate pastor with responsibilities for a large contemporary service. He says of his church:

> Our main struggle in introducing the POWR model was convincing our leaders that they needed to have a voice in the planning—in short, to see themselves as more than just drummers or guitarists or media creators, but as architects of communal worship, whose input is both needed and valued to create dynamic and authentic worship services. Taking time to make this cultural shift has helped our worship planners and team members feel

> more invested in worship, which pushes our creativity and our community orientation to higher and higher levels as everyone involved has bought into a new understanding of worship and their leadership therein.

Because a number of musicians rotate in and out of the worship leadership, this planning team is now actually several teams, each responsible—along with Jonathan, the primary preacher—for a different Sunday of the month. Recently Jonathan reported, "Now, a year and a half into using the model, we are really starting to see more and more cohesive services grounded in the Scripture and geared to the style, felt needs, and culture of our community." These planners, both youth and adult team members, are growing closer as their rehearsals evolve into discussions of Scripture texts and music—a liturgical jam session of planning.

*****

PLANNING TEAM: Rotating teams of musicians, led by the pastor.

SCOPE OF RESPONSIBILITY: Team members plan the services they will be leading (one per month).

SCHEDULE

Planning: As they begin rehearsals for their next service (three weeks out).

Ordering: By e-mail, with details finalized at the rehearsal before the Sunday they lead.

Reflecting: Lunch together after the service they lead, and extensive e-mail conversation.

*****

The Worship Committee Plans Special Services

Beth is the pastor of an older congregation whose members are mostly retired. The worship committee has many dedicated and longstanding members who give time and energy to their tasks of preparing the altar, deploying the usher teams, and giving practical assistance to the pastor in worship matters. Introducing the planning model for special services provided a way to re-energize the established committee. Beth reports:

> We engaged in exciting planning conversations for Holy Week services, particularly the Good Friday evening worship, which was very moving and spiritually engaged because of the depth of conversation in the planning group. The starting point was the Scripture texts and selection of passages that would interact meaningfully with anthems and other music. We were able to move past simply selecting hymns toward looking at Scripture passages alongside music, thinking about the meaning both intended to convey and how they could work together. We also planned visual images for the first time. Because the service was not a typical Sunday-morning order of worship, the planning team felt freedom and encouragement to make the service unique and to introduce new worship experiences. That service was our greatest triumph!

Building on that triumph and the enthusiasm it generated, the worship committee was expanded to include the artist who had designed the visuals for Holy Week and a member who had recently joined the church. The committee's main work continues to be the functional preparation of altar and sacrament and the recruiting of volunteers for worship leadership, but the members delight in planning special services throughout the year.

*****

PLANNING TEAM: Pastor, organist, six members of the worship committee (including chairs of altar guild and ushers, who coordinate and oversee practical details of the service).

SCOPE OF RESPONSIBILITY: Serves as the planning team for special services (Christmas Eve, Ash Wednesday, Holy Week).

LENGTH OF SERVICE: Two years (standard rotation for this denomination).

MEETING SCHEDULE:

Planning: One Wednesday-evening session two months before special service.

Ordering: Three weekly meetings before service.

Reflecting: One meeting following the service.

*****

Multiple Teams for Each Major Season

The pastors of a new church start developed this structure as a way to teach the parishioners about worship and quickly involve new members in the life of the congregation. Unlike the model above, this variation involves the team members mostly in the imaginative conversation around the text and the generation of ideas, not so much in concern for the details or preparation of the space. Pastor Matt explains:

> We have put the model in place for Advent, Lent, and Easter seasons with three to five people per team, one team per service. The most fruitful part was really the impact it had upon the people participating (roughly fifty-five) and the enthusiasm it generated. This model is helping us teach our parishioners why we worship the way we worship. We have found the teams to be an excellent short-term opportunity for new folks coming to the church who want to participate and meet others but who don't want a long-term commitment. I am beginning to teach other staff and laypeople how to lead a team, so that if we want to do this for every Sunday, I don't have to be at all the meetings.

The continued use of this structure has resulted in the involvement of more than two-thirds of the membership in liturgical planning. As new members join, they are quickly invited to become part of a seasonal team.

*****

PLANNING TEAM: Several teams of three to five people each.
SCOPE OF RESPONSIBILITY: Planning for one service.
LENGTH OF SERVICE: One season; one service.
SCHEDULE

Planning: One overview meeting, all teams for a particular season, at least two months before the start of the season. Then one meeting per team, Sunday evenings.

Ordering: By the staff in weekly meetings; each service ordered several weeks out.

Reflecting: By the team members after the service; by the staff in weekly meetings; by other congregants in Bible studies and Sunday-school classes.

*****

Pastor and Volunteers Plan throughout the Year

This model has worked in a variety of churches. The pastor of one midsize congregation explained:

> We plan further ahead with longer meetings of the pastors, music minister, and lay planning team several times a year (according to season, or the preaching minister's outline of a sermon series), which gives us direction and themes for music or visuals. And then we have more frequent and shorter meetings that deal with the ordering of the service and the fine-tuning and adjusting of the plan. This has reduced the overall load on both the pastors and the volunteers.

This structure takes advantage of regular staff planning already in place. Weekly staff meetings have been rejuvenated (and shortened), thanks to the ordering work of the team.

*****

PLANNING TEAM: Two pastors, music minister, six invited lay members.

SCOPE AND RESPONSIBILITY: Staff and volunteers plan the seasons in advance (e.g., in September for Advent and Christmas); planning team orders the service; staff is responsible for final details of the service. Volunteers schedule and train lay leaders for worship.

LENGTH OF SERVICE: Volunteers serve for one year.

SCHEDULE:

Planning: Four meetings per year to plan ahead for the upcoming season (two to three hours per meeting).

Ordering: Planning team meets monthly for one hour to order the upcoming services; staff meets weekly to complete the details.

Reflecting: As part of the planning meeting for the next season.

*****

Training the Team Members

People who volunteer, or who accept an invitation to join a working group, want to believe that they can meet the expectations of the task. They want to be equipped, to do well, and to participate in a meaningful experience. How will you prepare and train the planning team members in your parish? Two experiences from local parishes may be helpful as you determine what is required for your team.

Let the Learning Unfold through the Practice

The best preparation is a desire to learn and to be open to God's Word, to be attentive and to be present. Pastor Matt says:

> The most important thing is what happens to the people as they work in the planning process; that is our focus. For our new congregation there is a huge learning curve in the ordering (why we do what we do and how). The planning comes pretty naturally and fosters new relationships between individuals. People have to grow into their roles, and as they participate in the planning, they are being trained; they learn more and more about how what we do shapes our faith and life.

Matt's comments point to the catechetical opportunity; teaching is a natural part of the team structure. "Why do we do what we do?" is a fundamental question about worship and about who the congregation is in this place and as a part of the larger church. Over time, as he leads and as the questions arise, the pastor will teach about historical patterns of worship, the seasons, and sacramental practice. This is a conversational learning experience that is immediately put into practice: "Now I see why we sing these words." "I had always wondered about the use of this color."

Conduct Regularly Scheduled Classes to Prepare the Planners

Short-term classes, regular weekly Bible studies, or classes on congregational song can become the foundational preparation for the worship planners.

Kevin, a student pastor, used a denominational study guide on Holy Communion as the curriculum for a Sunday-evening class in his rural congregation. The participants, some of whom were lifelong members of the church, were excited to connect their own feasting at the table with people in the earliest Christian gatherings, and to discover the meaning of words and gestures they had long practiced but never considered deeply. They were eager to share their new understanding with the whole congregation. The pastor took advantage of the congregation's desire for knowledge and its longing to experience a richer sacramental practice, and began weekly celebration of Holy Communion.

The next step was Kevin's inviting the class members to become a planning team for the Lenten season. The curiosity and confidence generated from the Sunday-evening sessions were nourished into leadership that has revitalized the congregation's worship.

Knowing the Team Members: Spiritual Types

As you organize the teams, you may choose to schedule an orientation session. Many of the team members will know one another; they have sung in the choir, played on the softball team, served as ushers or preschool teachers, attended a Bible study together. Some team members have recently joined the congregation and are eager to find new friends. In various gatherings and circumstances, both inside and outside the church, they all have introduced themselves, often by their family identities, their roles on committees, their hobbies, or their work in the world. In the ministry of planning worship, they may come to know one another in more deeply spiritual ways. As the team forms for its ministry of planning, you can help the members discover their "heart language"—the ways in which they know and speak of God.

A number of inventories or tools can help people discover and understand the spiritual dimensions of their personalities. We found professor and pastoral counselor Corinne Ware's small book *Discover Your Spiritual Type* particularly helpful. Building on work in Christian spirituality by Urban T. Holmes, Ware presents her understanding of spiritual types—that is, the primary ways in which people appropriate their knowledge of God and prefer to express it in worship. She speaks of the "dis-ease" of worshipers who have a "deep inner sense that their natural tendencies are either being violated by present worship patterns or simply not being allowed expression by those practices."[1] Ware describes four basic spiritual types with corresponding worship needs. While the types are fluid, the distinctions do explain, and can help worship planners accept and provide, a range of expressions for all who worship. In identifying their spiritual type, or a combination of several types, members of a group can see their own worship preferences not as personal quirks but as a significant part of their identity. And in knowing and affirming themselves, they can know and affirm others as they work together.

The spiritual typologies are laid out in a circle with quadrants formed by two intersecting lines. The end points of the vertical line are, in Ware's terminology, "intellectual" and "heartfelt." These points describe how one "goes about knowing—through the activity of the rational mind or by accessing feelings."[2] The end points of the horizontal line are, in Ware's terms, "imaging" and "mystery." This line helps define how people conceptualize their understanding of God—whether God is revealed and known and often described in concrete terms, or whether God is mystery, the unknowable. The quadrants formed by the two intersecting lines—the spaces where our own ways of knowing and the ways we understand and conceptualize the Holy come together—define the various spiritual types.

Briefly, here are Ware's four spiritual types, and some characteristics of each.

Type I: Head Spirituality

Type I, in the upper-right quadrant formed by "intellectual" and "imaging," describes people who want to know God intellectually. Their images of God and the ways in which they speak of their faith are highly affected by words—by preaching (a good sermon is essential) and by carefully chosen hymn texts. They want to be challenged with phrases from hymns or a sermon they can mull over during the week. Good worship is ordered, sticks to the plan, and moves the worshiper through the service with no distractions or disruptions. In coming to receive the sacrament of Holy Communion, the people of this spiritual type prefer to be directed from their seats to the altar or kneeling rail. They appreciate the choir's anthem offered on their behalf, the procession of the clergy and choir. They participate best in an order of worship that they know deeply and that is essentially the same week to week.

Type II: Heart Spirituality

This type is found in the lower-right quadrant of the circle, in the portion formed by "heartfelt" and "imaging." People with heart spirituality gauge the authenticity of worship by the way the experience feels to them. In their prayer language, they prefer personal names for God and concrete, tangible phrases: "Father," "friend," "my personal Savior." The people of heart spirituality want a sermon that inspires, transforms, "convicts and converts." They want, in the words of Doris Akers's hymn "Sweet, Sweet Spirit," to "have been revived when we shall leave this place."[3] When they come to receive the sacrament of Holy Communion, they may wish to remain at the altar rail and not to be directed. While singing the hymn stanzas in sequence is important, it is imperative that there be freedom to repeat a refrain or to continue the music under the words of a prayer. There is a stronger attention to the immediate movement of the Spirit than to the order of service on the page.

Type III: Mystic Spirituality

As indicated in the lower-left quadrant formed by "heartfelt" and "mystery," people in this third type know and experience God as "mystery" and may use that language to speak of God: "unknowable," "wind," "breath," "Holy One." They appreciate the repetitive music of Taizé, in which they may participate by singing or by allowing the music to flow around them. They welcome receiving Holy Communion in silence or with chant or songs led by a cantor. They need times of deep stillness and meditative prayer. They prefer a bidding prayer with silence for personal petitions rather than a long prayer spoken by one voice. People of this spiritual type do not need to focus on a lot of decor or seasonal altar designs; simple visuals are best.

Type IV: Kingdom Spirituality

In the upper-left quadrant, formed by "mystery" and "intellectual," are the "doers." Their work *is* their prayer. Worship strengthens and prepares them in concrete ways for the task of ministering in and to the world. They have a vision of justice and direct their energy toward bringing about God's reign in the world. They remind us to pray for the world, to consider the poor, and to work for justice. Announcements in worship should lift up opportunities for missions and service that makes a difference in the community. People of this spiritual type may understand the sacrament of Holy Communion as "food for the journey." They take to heart the words of the prayer after communion: "Send us out to do the work you have given us to do, to love and serve you as faithful witnesses of Christ our Lord."[4]

Celebrating the Diversity of Spiritual Types

As you read these descriptions, you may recognize people in your congregation. You probably see yourself in one or more of these descriptions. Most of us are inclined toward a particular spiritual type, though we have characteristics of more than one of the types. We are complex people.

When we explored Ware's four types in our staff meeting, we rejoiced together in the discoveries about ourselves and one another. In our small group were people who saw themselves in type I, the "head spirituality"; they needed an ordered space in which to center themselves and to hear God speak through the familiar hymns and historic liturgy. Others identified with spiritual type II, a "heart spirituality"; they knew God through the response of the heart, in extemporaneous prayers that used rhythmic cadences from hymns deep in their memory. They were the ones who often reminded us that we should just "let the Spirit flow" and not watch the clock so closely.

These revelations, rather than giving us cause to defend our "type," gave us a mysterious freedom to claim our individual identities and to affirm and allow space for the other. Our team immediately felt more whole, more complete. The biblical affirmation "there are many gifts but the same Spirit" came alive in our midst. The conversation was balanced with voices and opinions from every spiritual perspective. We used the results of the spiritual type inventory to develop planning teams with diverse membership, pairing very different spiritual types, making space for all voices to be heard. We are learning from and working with those who stretch us beyond ourselves, who can expand our individual inclinations and preferences with a broader range of song and prayer and gesture in worship.

In the ensuing planning conversations, we began to pay closer attention to the balance of sound and silence and to language and visuals that brought the concerns of the world and the call to mission into the worship space. We began to incorporate both the brief songs of the heart and more elaborate strophic hymns. We learned many songs in new languages, so that we might join the prayer of the world. We did not practice these gestures of care and inclusion so that more people would attend worship or "like" the services, but because we began to understand more profoundly that those who worshiped beside us were multifaceted people, created and creative, longing to give expression to praise and awe and thanks and lament. Making space for their songs is central to the ministry of the planning teams.

As you give close attention to forming a planning team, as you invite members into the circle of this ministry, as you become more aware of the diversity within the group, and as the members become acquainted with one another and begin their conversation, expect a "new thing" to appear. You and the members of the team will be learning a new language together, a language that is more descriptive and poetic and sensory. You will be exploring biblical texts, hymns and songs, prayers and visual ideas. You will learn more about the traditions of the church, and more about one another. And you will invite the congregation to participate in the renewed worship that results from your ministry. The outcome of the conversational planning is a hoped-for but yet-unrealized possibility that will take shape as God's Spirit is at work among you. You will be amazed by insights and energy, by moments of discovery and revelation. God's own creative work in and through the planning team will be surprising and life-giving.

Let's begin this holy work.

Chapter 4

Planning

A Conversation with the Biblical Text

Bethel Church's worship planning team met for the first time on a Saturday morning in January. It was early, and the weather was damp and cold, but the coffee was ready, and the classroom where the members gathered was bright and warm. Someone noted that it was awfully soon after Christmas to be thinking about Holy Week, but Pastor Dave had said the group needed time to prepare. He had chatted with most of the team members individually or in pairs and had explained his vision for celebrating an Easter Vigil this year. He had already sent each of them an explanation of the Vigil—telling them about lighting the new Paschal candle and entering the church in procession, about the Scripture readings that told the whole salvation story, and about the baptism of new members. Most of the team members had not known of this historic service, though their little town always had a community Easter sunrise service in the park. But as Dave talked about the earliest Christian communities and read from some early church writings, the members were convinced that entering the whole Christian story through the celebration of the Great Vigil would be a profound event for their congregation.

As the planning team meets to begin its work, whether for a single Sunday or a season, the members become part of a wider circle of the faithful who have prepared for the gathering of believers in other places and times. In *Christian Assembly: Marks of the Church in a Pluralistic Age,* liturgical theologian Gordon Lathrop writes:

> The catholic church . . . is always a local meeting, local people using local language, locally prepared food, local water sources.

> But it is always a local meeting gathered before and enlivened by the one God. Its words, food and water are used with biblical and Christian eschatological intent. And, because God is the central actor here, this local assembly will always be itself opening onto and participating in the one assembly of God of every time and every place.[1]

When the pastor or planning-group leader gives attention to this reality, the planners are centered for their work of making space here and now for the Spirit of God, in the fullness of word and sacrament, praise and prayer. A wider perspective puts this local team in the company of ministers in other places. As the planners engage in the imaginative work of listening to the text, they are actively remembering their own story and its intersection with God's story, told again and again.

Leading the Conversation

Members of the congregation may serve as leaders of the worship planning teams, but when the conversational model is being introduced and integrated into the congregation, the work is best guided by the pastor or the minister of worship. After the pattern of conversation and the planning groups are established, the pastor may train emerging leaders for this work. Whether a lay member or pastor, the facilitator of the planning team needs a caring spirit of discernment in guiding the conversation, reflecting what has been said, asking follow-up questions for clarity, and inviting and including each person's thoughts and ideas.

Planning-team members will need some time to become comfortable with the process, especially if they are accustomed to working in a more task-oriented way or see the work of the worship team primarily as preparing for the sacraments or scheduling the acolytes. As you will recall from the discussion of spiritual types in chapter 3, those who are "head spirituality" types may find this conversation challenging. They will be more concerned with the meaning and the truth of the text than with imagining. They may urge the process along, wanting to get the ideas organized.

However, for those in other quadrants of the spiritual-types circle—for example, those who thrive on conceptual and abstract thinking about the biblical text—the conversation will be freeing. All members of the team will need to grow in trusting one another and the process. The leader, while facilitating the discussion, must be careful not to crowd the conversation with words, but to allow moments of silence for the words of the text to echo in the room and in the minds of the planners, to give time for ideas to form and for the planners to reflect.

Space for Meeting

Ideally, the conversation unfolds with the members seated around a table or in a circle of chairs. All the voices on the team need to be heard, and a circular arrangement makes a hospitable place for seeing and speaking to one another. In our location, we sit in a circle of comfortable chairs in the center of which is a large goatskin drum. The drum itself serves as metaphor for our work. When people are hesitant or ideas are bogging down, we often say, "Put it on the drum," meaning, "You don't have to explain your thoughts or defend that idea; just put your words out with all the other words in this welcoming space." Some of the thoughts expressed may even seem contradictory, but in the circle all ideas are encouraged and held without judgment. In any working group, one personality can dominate or overpower those who are more introspective or reticent. Or participants may defer to the leader as the expert or authority, especially if that person is speaking from the front of the room or the head of the table. A circular seating arrangement can help mediate both these tendencies and keep the conversation moving among all the members.

Resources and Preparation

Before the planning session, the leader should send team members the texts (whether from the lectionary or chosen by the preacher) for the services on which they will be working. If the texts have been read before the session, the planners will be ready to read aloud and to listen carefully as the conversation proceeds.

Besides preparing a space and sending the texts, you will want to gather planning resources—several copies of your denominational hymnal, hymnals and songbooks from other traditions, books of prayers, Bibles in one or two translations, plenty of blank paper, and colored markers. We also use books like *Prepare!* (cited in the list of resources on page 137), in which all the lectionary texts for each Sunday are printed. Or you might print the texts from an online source.

The leader should have a working familiarity with the resources the group might use—the structure of the denomination's hymnal and book of worship, the indexes and contents—and know how to access helpful online resources quickly. Such knowledge can keep the conversation moving as the group makes suggestions for songs or prayers or other liturgical expressions. The bibliography at the end of this book lists many published resources and websites, based primarily on the Revised Common Lectionary.

An ongoing exploration of resources fosters a spirit of curiosity and a sense of discovery as the group uncovers new hymn texts or finds prayers for particular circumstances or celebrations. Especially if the team is meeting to plan for a whole season, the leader may wish to take time to offer an overview of materials for those Sundays. Or the music director may introduce seasonal hymns or a new collection of songs to stimulate interest in all the possibilities.

Process

Unless the team is meeting for an extended time to plan services for an entire season, the planning session is a prayerful (and playful) conversation that lasts about one hour. Attempting to complete the process in less time will make participants feel rushed, and the discussion will be too compressed. If you spend much more than an hour, the conversation will drag or wander beyond the texts and themes at hand.

The following outline will guide you through this hour. The times are approximate. Sometimes you may need more time to ponder the texts; at other times the team may move quickly to brainstorming ideas. Appendix B offers a leader's guide for the planning session.

Gather with Prayer (5 minutes)

Those in the group are coming from the sundry activities of their day. Take a few minutes to gather thanksgivings and concerns. Do some catching up. If this is the first meeting of a new team, allow time for welcome and introductions. Then move into the readings with a brief prayer for illumination:

Let us pray:
O God, you spoke your Word and the world was created;
send us your Spirit in this hour, that through the reading of your Word
and through our conversation and study,
our listening and speaking, our wondering and discerning,
we might hear you speak a new word to us and to your people in this place;
through Christ who is the Word, who is the Truth, who is our Life. Amen.

As you begin, select a person to take notes or to serve as scribe, using a whiteboard or a large computer screen, so that all the ideas are visible. After the meeting, the scribe will e-mail the notes to team members and the pastor and music director. One team with which we are acquainted meets around a table covered with large sheets of paper. As the members read the texts, and images and ideas come to mind, they write or draw on the paper in front of them. At the end of the session the scribe collects the paper, organizes those jottings, and sends them around.

Introduce the Season (5 minutes)

If this is a session to outline themes for an entire season, give a brief introduction. For example, if you are planning for the Lenten season, talk a bit about the historic emphasis on final instruction of the catechumens preparing for baptism, or give a brief overview of the trajectory of the Gospel texts as we journey toward Jerusalem. If you are meeting to plan a particular Sunday, locate it within the season. Are you planning within the Easter season, moving toward Pentecost and the birth of the church? Is this Sunday part of the long season of Ordinary Time or the Sundays after Pentecost? Are there local celebrations that will factor into the preparations? For example, will there be baptisms or confirmations on Pentecost? Will the children from the vacation Bible school be singing on the third Sunday in June? It is within these contexts that the Scripture will be read.

Hear the Texts Read (10 minutes)

If your congregation uses the Revised Common Lectionary and hears all the assigned texts each week, read the particular Sunday's texts aloud, using a different reader for each. Invite the group to listen without looking at the text. Then hear the Gospel (or the preaching text) again, read by a different voice as the planners follow the printed text. Allow the words to sound in the space; don't rush this step. Do not comment on the texts, but allow time for silent reflection. In this meditative time, invite the team members to write down key words or to quickly draw a picture of the text.

Phase I: Thinking about the Text (10 minutes)

After a brief pause, you are ready to begin a conversation that engages the team's emotional and affective responses to the text. The first set of questions invites personal reflections; there is no correct answer. Not all the questions that follow will be applicable to every text. You will think of other questions or ways to stimulate creative engagement with the story.

1. What words and phrases do you hear when the text is read aloud? What images are evoked? What surprised you? How does this text make you feel? What emotions are generated? Are you confused? Comforted? Angry? Sad?
2. What do you see as this text is read? For example, in the story of the healing of the paralytic, what is the weather like? Or in the postresurrection appearance beside the Sea of Galilee, what color is the sky?

3. If you close your eyes, what can you smell? The fish on the fire by the seashore? The dingy clothing on the blind man by the side of the road?
4. What do you hear? Is it quiet? Noisy? What is the mood of the primary character or the narrator?
5. What is the texture of the reading? Is it smooth? Jagged? Rough?

This conversation is not about facts or right answers; it is evocative, poetic, and affective. The intent, as one pastor says, is "to ask a series of questions aimed at creating a picture of what the text is saying to members of the group, so that the words begin to live—becoming a moving part of the whole story."

If the text comes from the series of readings for a season, then questions about themes or directions within the entire season can arise. For example, the Old Testament readings for the Sundays in Advent move toward the promised birth of the Messiah, beginning with the prophetic texts that speak of the end time, the second coming of Christ. After the group has read those texts in sequence, as suggested above, the particular text for this day can then be heard and considered as a part of the larger seasonal trajectory. Team members might comment, "As I heard this lesson, there seems to be a big shift from the lesson we heard last week." The questions about color or light or texture are helpful in articulating themes. "Last week's text seemed jagged and rocky; this one is smoother, more level. It's greener."

The scribe will take notes on all that is said. At this point, the words may be scattered across the page or the screen, but as the conversation continues, possible themes will emerge, and concepts and colors will begin to connect and make sense.

The beauty of the "P" [planning] session is to find that guiding metaphor or image in the text. The use of image and metaphor allowed us to be united around something in a way that one reading of a text might not—multiple possibilities that one particular interpretation might not have had. I think the thing that helps our

> personalities work well together is that we're open, accepting, and polite. And despite our differences we all have this: We haven't invested in any of the things that come out of our mouths until the group has invested in them. If you're too invested in what you speak during the "P," the process could come to a halt.
>
> —RANDALL, PLANNING TEAM MEMBER

Focusing on a Theme (5 minutes)

The facilitator should bring closure to the initial conversation, so that group members are ready to listen to a brief statement about the direction of the sermon.

Talking about the sermon too early can push some of the quieter voices to the margins in favor of the "expert" voice of the preacher. But having heard the range of responses (and in that hearing, having learned more about the people who will listen and respond to the sermon), the pastor can relate these responses to the season, the background of the texts, and ways she already is starting to think about weaving the message into the congregational context. The balance of power in the circle can be at stake in this moment. If the preacher talks too much or is too set on the exact unfolding of the sermon, the process may collapse in favor of her authority and expertise. Planners will begin to feel that their ideas have no merit, and the conversation may fade. If the preacher is too uncertain or not forthcoming or helpful, then the process can veer off in random directions. Guiding the conversation requires spiritual discernment and skill—careful listening and reflecting back, knowing when to nudge the conversation with another question or to move in a new direction.

The process of integrating the group's initial affective responses with the sermon theme is guided by the question "What is God's message for us on this day as we gather to praise, to listen, to respond in offering and feast, and to be sent as the church into the world?" Words and phrases from the group's responses will overlap or come together with the focus for the sermon. You can note points of similarity or opposition, helpful insights, and articulate phrases. The scribe will assist in visually connecting the emotional responses and the sermon's direction as he listens to the conversation and circles certain responses or phrases, joins others with a line or two, and moves less related responses to a secondary list or off the page.

Phase 2: Concrete Ideas (15 minutes)

When the team has responded to the texts, heard the preacher's initial thoughts and direction, and given focus to the message of the service, members move in the next step to express more concrete ideas. Appendix B has two options for recording the ideas from this discussion: by category (music, visuals, prayers, etc.) or within the general order of the service (gathering, hearing, etc.). Whichever option you choose, the guiding question for the team is: "How can we give expression to this Word in the worship service?"

1. What sounds do you hear in the worship service this day? Is the music lively? Contemplative? Festive? Reflective? Do you hear silence? From where do the sounds emanate? Are there readers scattered around the space? A voice from the balcony? Do particular hymns and songs come to mind?
2. What gestures and movements are summoned by our reading of the texts? A solemn procession? Dancing? Moving to the altar rail for prayer?
3. How do the texts help us imagine the arrangement of the physical space in which we will worship? What visual expressions are suggested? Shall we leave the wilting palms in the aisles? Should we move the altar table to the center of the space?

In this step the preacher's thoughts, the team members' responses to the text, and the questions "what?" and "how?" are in dialogue. Some people will see things: an arrangement on the altar table or in the deep windowsills reflecting the meaning of the text, or the children bringing the offering forward. Others will hear the choir or congregation singing, the sounds of organ or other instruments, phrases of hymn texts, the words of the prayers, the text read in different languages. Some will look through the hymnal and songbooks for inspiration; others will peruse books of prayers. Invite multiple responses: "Maybe we could have three readers." "Could we bring the Gospel to life with drama, or a readers' theatre?" "What hymns and songs might help us express the theme of the texts?" Encourage everyone to enter the conversation.

As the planners become more experienced with the process and more familiar with additional resources, the planning sessions will become livelier and more complex. One song from the global church sung in worship will elicit questions about other possibilities and sources. The offer of freshly baked bread for communion will soon become a regularly accepted gift.

> We put a big white piece of paper on the table, and everybody had crayons. We read the Scripture, and then we brainstormed. We all wrote on the paper—words and pictures, whatever came to mind. It was a community effort, so all our ideas were out there together. We talked while we were writing, an ongoing conversation. We'd write, and then we'd go back to the text. And then we started to think about songs and whether the theme and the music would lift or uphold the text. It was great! I think because of the creativity and the freedom of expression, God was allowed to move in the services; it left the door open for the Spirit of God to work.
>
> —Cezanne, team member

Completing the Planning (5 minutes)

Now the discussion begins to move from the possibilities toward the ordering.

1. Ask if there are any additional thoughts or ideas; then summarize the discussion.
2. Review the suggested hymns and songs, particular prayers or litanies, and ideas for processions, dancers, or visual designs.

3. Assign tasks. Whom do we need to contact to help make these ideas come alive? What gifts and talents do we need? How will we divide up this work?
4. Outline a clear reporting process. If this team is handing off the planning notes to the staff, by what date will that happen? "We need to know by next Thursday whether . . ."
5. End with a brief prayer of thanks for the gifts of God's Word, our creative powers, and the inspiration of the Spirit in our midst.

After the meeting, the scribe will organize the notes and send them to the pastor, the music director, and members of the team. Clear and concise notes are especially important if the people engaged in the creative brainstorming and planning are not those who will complete the ordering of the service.

Summary

The initial planning session centers on the themes drawn from the scriptural texts for the day and the responses to them. Participants ask, "What is God's word for us this day, and how shall we give expression to that word in worship?" In this session:

1. The planners gather. They select a scribe.
2. The pastor/leader introduces the season.
3. The group reads the texts.
4. The group responds, led by affective and sensory questions.
5. The pastor/preacher gives a brief overview of the sermon direction.
6. Planners brainstorm specific ideas for music, prayer, visuals, and spatial design.
7. The session ends with a reiteration of the plans thus far and assignment of tasks in preparation for ordering the service.
8. The scribe collects all the ideas and after the meeting sends the notes to the team members, the music director, and the preaching pastor.

As the hour concludes, all the team members are enthusiastically looking ahead. The lay members of the team might depart with new questions about particular elements of worship or about the liturgical season or the texts for the day. They have been encouraged by the group's acceptance of their suggestions. They look forward to sending a few e-mails or making a phone call to invite others to offer their gifts to make the Word come alive in the service. Staff or clergy will also be thinking of specific decisions and choices to be made. The music director will be considering the rehearsal time available (or required) for the suggested hymns, any new service music, and the repertoire already in the choir folders. But having been a part of the planning conversation, she will have new insights into both the biblical texts and the spiritual and musical needs of the congregation. And likewise, the pastor, having been surprised by a part of the text he had not even noticed, will be drawn into further study by stimulating questions.

The Word of God is alive among the people; the message of that Word is taking form. In the next session, the team will put the worship service in order.

Chapter 5

Ordering

Decisions and Details

Pastor Ed had left the planning meeting with a page of notes. Using these and the additional ideas sent around by Charlotte, the scribe for the team, Ed was now working his way through a long list of hymn suggestions, ideas for a seasonal display in the entrance, and plans for carrying the Bible into the center aisle and reading the Gospel in the midst of the congregation. That was new! They had never had a Gospel procession here. But after someone made the suggestion, and Ed agreed that bringing the Word to "dwell among us" was a powerful gesture, everyone got excited, and the ideas coalesced around the theme of the text. Now, preparing for the ordering session, Pastor Ed was encouraged. He had not imagined that the team would get this enthusiastic about planning. In the next session, they would meet to tend to the details—making decisions about the music and the flow of the service, and assigning the tasks of bringing the Word to dwell in their midst.

Leading the Conversation

Ordering the worship service is a much more concrete process than planning. While still imagining the sounds and sights and actions of the approaching worship service, the planners move from the brainstorming of the previous session to more detailed thinking. Ordering involves decisions and lists and preparation of the space and leaders. The practical discussion concerns content, personnel, and logistics. The *ordo* is established; the ordering process enlivens the structure with the elements of expression for this day. Nate, pastor of a newly formed congregation, explains:

> Our worship has a structure. We will always engage in these four actions: Gathering, Hearing God's Word in Scripture, Responding (especially in Communion) and Sending Forth. These actions will always occur. However, within that structure, we can be somewhat creative with the language, images, postures, and gestures that we choose for leaders and the people. These foci are the work of the planning team.

The central actions of the service around the font, the book, and the table form us in our identity in Christ. The specific congregational expressions in word and song and prayer, and the flow of the whole service are the variables to which we will give attention in the ordering conversation. The relevant questions at this juncture are: What do we need in order to give full expression to the Word of God in this gathering? How can the flow of the service make space for the Spirit of God? These are questions of "which" and "who" and "why" and "how."

A multisensory worship service provides a place for all the people who will gather to sing, pray, listen, and respond. Those who long for silence, those who want careful order and progression, those who want spontaneity, those who come to remember the world and its needs as they prepare for service—all need to find a welcome, and a language in which they can participate. When the planning team represents all spiritual types (see chapter 3), there is greater likelihood that the worship service will offer a multiplicity of invitations and expressions. Pay attention to all the voices in the circle as you gather for this work.

Preparing to Meet

Listening to the diverse voices is critical as you refine the ideas and choose hymns, songs, prayers, and other elements in the service. Depending on the model you appropriate for the process, the planners who generated the ideas may not be physically present for the ordering session. If this is the case in your congregation, listen for the echoes of the previous conversation as the group orders the service. You recall that the two most straightforward options for ordering the service are

1. One team continues its work from planning through the worship service itself; and
2. An initial planning team hands off the creative notes to the staff, which completes the order of service and coordinates lay leadership in the worship service.

Whichever structure (or variation) your congregation adopts, the ordering process is the same.

Having space between the planning/brainstorming and the ordering/defining phases allows some ideas to float away and others to rise in importance. The quick responses in the brainstorming meeting have done their work of spurring other thoughts. Planners have also had time to attend to assignments and report on the progress. However, if too much time passes between planning and ordering, the ideas lose momentum and enthusiasm wanes. More complex services like the Easter Vigil require plenty of time for planning, ordering, and rehearsing. However, we have learned that preparing the final order of the weekly worship about a week after the initial planning and at least a week before the worship service keeps the ideas sharp and gives time for final detailed preparation.

You will likely also make use of online conversations between meetings to update one another on the progress of writing prayers or of recruiting additional readers or communion servers. Music directors can keep the team apprised of available musicians. ("Brad will be home from college this week, and I invited him to play trumpet on the opening hymn and at the offertory. We'll want to take full advantage of his talents, so of the hymns suggested, look especially at 'I Sing the Almighty Power of God' and 'Sing Praise to God Who Reigns Above,' and we can make the final decision when we meet.") Members of the planning team can report on their assignments ("Amanda is excited that we asked her to dance, and she has begun working on the choreography for the Pentecost procession"). While e-mail offers a good way to share information or send encouragement, the group may attempt to make too many binding decisions about the service via e-mail exchanges, not realizing that one person did not read the messages going around or that another fell out of the loop. The face-to-face meeting is crucial to the continued conversation.

In preparing for the meeting, the scribe should send a reminder to team members, asking them to read the preaching text again, review the notes and ideas sent after the planning meeting, and complete any assignments. The ordering meeting will last about one hour. After initial decision-making, the group may break up into twos and threes to work on details, such as putting the bulletin in final form or crafting the petitions and intercessions.

If the team always meets in the same space, leaders can more easily ensure that needed resources will be at hand. Because final music selection is a large part of this ordering session, and some members of the team may not be trained to read music or to recall quickly the sound of a hymn or song, planners will also appreciate access to a piano or electronic keyboard. Rather than hearing the musician's description of the song ("It's a strong, bright tune"), the team members can hear it for themselves. Everyone has the same experience and can participate in the discussion.

> Being ordered and intentional in the process allowed us to step back and literally see a worship service take form. The process was amazing—all the ideas were laid out, and then we picked up what was good, what we needed, and shaped it like clay on a potter's wheel. It was joyous; it was hard work. We had to discern what would work, what would be inclusive, what might be exclusive. Watching it come together was transformative for me.
>
> —CEZANNE, PLANNING TEAM MEMBER

Making Decisions

Ordering the service is a decision-making task. The team is involved in making choices; from many fine ideas, team members will select the best and most appropriate expressions for this day.

Many decisions are dictated by available resources and options. Two violins would sound lovely on this hymn, but we have a clarinet player. Other decisions are based on the needed preparation time. The idea for ribbon banners may need to move from the Easter season until Pentecost, a shift that allows time to construct them properly.

For each ordering session, the main decisions will involve the congregational music, the reading of Scripture, and the prayers. Choosing hymns can become an exercise in the selection of familiar favorites or what is new in a particular musical genre. So, too, suggestions for the presentation of Scripture may be novel but not grounded in the text.

We often choose from what we know or have experienced; our preferences are usually drawn from styles and patterns that appeal to us. However, we need both familiar and new hymns and songs; we sing our heritage and learn new languages to join in praise with the worldwide community. We need to present the text in new ways to make the Word come alive for all ages in the assembly through clear and articulate reading; through drama, mime, or dance. We need a wide range of prayer languages and gestures: standing, sitting, kneeling, moving, hands raised or folded; silent prayers, spoken petitions, prayers for one voice. Selecting from the many possibilities suggested in the planning session requires making informed and careful choices. The pastor in charge and the music minister can make some arbitrary decisions, and at times may need to. But as they are leading the people into deeper and more participatory worship, the planning team members themselves are becoming better equipped to do this work.

Selecting the Music

Of the dozen or so congregational songs suggested in the initial planning session, four or five may have a place in this service; others may wait until another time. The following commentary and questions can guide the team in evaluating and selecting hymns and songs for the whole congregation and can help the team move beyond personal preference into a conversation that is more inclusive and inviting. The worshiping assembly itself will be assisted in offering praise and prayer and will be challenged and shaped by the range of styles sung.

READ THE TEXT OF THE HYMN OR SONG

1. How well does the text reflect the theme of the service? (Look especially at the interior stanzas of the hymn.) Where might it fit in this liturgy?
2. How does this hymn assist in telling the whole of the Christian story? Law and gospel, redemption and grace? Who is included?
3. What are the biblical references or images of God? Does the text expand our understanding and experience of God's saving work in our lives and in the world?
4. In the repertoire of hymns and songs we sing, do we express the fullness of awe and wonder, confession and pardon, thanksgiving and a call to service?
5. Who is the author of the text? As we look back over the season, is our congregation singing hymns by both men and women, from a range of time periods, from a wide geographic area?
6. Does the text stretch us? Does it strengthen us? Is the poetry interesting? Are the metaphors compelling?

LISTEN TO THE TUNE

1. What words describe the "feel" of this tune (majestic, contemplative, flowing, ballad-like, dancelike)?
2. Is it interesting? Does the melody flow in a lyric or majestic way, or is it static and repetitive?
3. Does the tune fit the text? Do the accents of the poetic phrases move smoothly with the tune? Does the pairing of text and tune reinforce the mood of both?
4. How singable is the tune? Will the congregation be able to sing it, or should the choir or soloists sing it? Can we learn it quickly, or do we need to rehearse it before the service?
5. Does this tune expand the congregation's range of musical styles and genres? Over time are we stretching to learn new hymns and songs?

6. What musical leadership is required? Organ? Piano or electronic keyboard? Guitar or band? Rhythm or percussion instruments?

These questions encourage conversation and discovery. As the planners learn to ask similar questions, they will become more curious about finding and exploring new resources, and may suggest: "We need to look for a hymn that expresses our longing for renewal." Or: "As we move to pray for the world, could the choir sing a song in another language?"

> Worshiping in our church has completely spoiled me! I have gotten used to having the songs relate to the Scripture texts and to the pastor's message. I never realized how important this is to me until I visited another congregation. All through that service, I kept thinking, "Why are we singing this? It doesn't have anything to do with the theme of the message."
>
> —SHEILA, MEMBER OF A MIDSIZE CONGREGATION

Reading the Word in the Assembly

One of the central actions in Christian worship is the reading and hearing of biblical texts. While the normal practice is to hear the text read clearly and articulately by one voice, close study of the text may suggest an expanded practice—a dramatic presentation, a readers' theater, or singing a hymn that paraphrases and parallels the text. Consider these questions:

1. What kind of text is this: narrative, parable, letter, teaching, prophecy, poetry?
2. What kind of oral reading (or musical expression) will best deliver the text and this genre? Drama? A choral reading with several voices? A narrator and dancers? Stanzas of a hymn woven into the spoken text?
3. How will we be prepared to hear the sermon that will follow?
4. Who will lead us? From what location?

Crafting and Selecting Prayers

The public prayers—whether extemporaneous, from a denominational prayer book, from an online source, or written by the pastor or a layperson—are the words the assembly speaks to God, collectively or through the voice of the leader. Selecting and crafting those words is holy work. The bibliography suggests books that are helpful in the writing of prayers, litanies, and other spoken elements of the service, along with several books of prayers related to the Revised Common Lectionary. The planning team's familiarity with and use of these resources will help enrich the vocabulary of prayer in the worship service. Questions for discussion and decision might include:

1. Is someone writing the prayers for this Sunday? Are we using prayers from a printed or online source?
2. Could we use some of the phrases from the opening hymn in the call to worship that precedes it?
3. Could we adapt the petitions suggested in our denominational resource to include images from the psalm for the day?
4. How do the words of the prayers reflect the metaphorical language of the Scripture and hymns?
5. How do the prayers in this worship service reflect the need for times of silence? Can people voice their petitions aloud?
6. Whose voices are heard in prayer? Only the pastor's? Lay leaders'? Deacons'?
7. Will the people stand or kneel?
8. Will they be speaking or singing a response to the petitions?
9. Is the language of the prayers direct and clear? If the assembly is reading the prayer together, is the language accessible to all ages and abilities?

Through discussion guided by the questions above, members of the planning team will grow in their understanding that what we sing and say in worship does matter. We express our faith together before God; we grow in faith as we are stretched by texts and tunes and thoughtful prayer language.

Expanding the Order of Worship

I know many churches in which, over time, elements of the liturgy have been diminished or eliminated, until the basic structure includes few Scripture readings, only one or two congregational songs, and not much additional congregational participation at all. With a new planning process and an expanded conversation between the pastor and lay members of the team, the established order of worship in your congregation may begin to seem cramped and tight. This is a good sign; you are growing into a new thing! You may need a new wineskin for the new wine of renewed worship. Use this discovery as a teaching and learning opportunity for you and your congregation. (The bibliography lists some teaching resources.)

Christina, a student pastor, reports:

> At first our team was working from our established order of worship, in which the congregation participated in essentially three hymns, the doxology, and a closing song of blessing, but we knew our people desired more. After studying the worship outline in our denomination's book of worship, we began to add more music and prayers for the whole congregation. Our choir learned the sung responses for the Great Thanksgiving, and soon the whole congregation was joining in. A few weeks ago one member asked if the congregation could speak their own petitions during the prayers of the people. I realized that over these few months we had not only expanded the congregation's participation, but we had invited them to claim their role in the liturgy. It's been an exciting renewal for our worship.

If you perceive the need for an expanded order of the liturgy, Appendix C includes an order of worship based on the liturgy historically used in many traditions, with some options for greater congregational participation. See how this order flows as a dialogue between hearing and responding, between listening for God and responding to God. Many congregations use this full order each week. You may not choose to adopt every element, and not all the rituals apply to every congregation. Some items receive attention for each service: the selection of music, the reading of texts, the prayers. Other practices might change seasonally. Lent might involve a sung *Kyrie* each week and more silence in the prayers for the world. During Advent you may add a ritual for lighting the Advent wreath. In the Easter season alleluias may bracket the reading of the Gospel.

As you become experienced with the conversational model for worship planning, you and the planners will begin to imagine small changes or inclusions that will enrich the service. You will see ways to expand the order, to flesh out the congregation's full participation in the liturgy. You will also become more conversant in the language of the questions, moving beyond a vocabulary of the preferential and familiar to consideration of all the people who will gather to worship—children, older members who may have diminished sight, those whose mobility is impaired, those with hearing loss, those who are visiting for the first time.

The Ordering Process

Equipped with the ideas generated in the planning session and with the spacious *ordo* and its possibilities, the team gathers for the work of ordering the service. It is helpful to work from the service outline or script so that you can see which elements are consistent from one service to the next and thus already in place, and which will require decisions and choices this time.

Gather with Prayer (3 minutes)

Come together with prayer for one another, the congregation, and your ministry of preparing this service of worship.

Let us pray:
O God, you have formed us each in mysterious and wonderful ways,
with diversity of mind and spirit,
of language and culture, of preference and expression,
and you have given us the community of fellowship in the church.

Give us in this hour the gift of your guiding Spirit,
that in our decisions and choices we might be mindful of all who will gather for worship, lifting one great song of praise to You. Amen.

Review and Report (5 minutes)

Review the texts and sermon synopsis to reinforce the theme of the service. Note any additions to the service. Will new members be joining the church? Is there a baptism?

Report on any previous assignments that will affect the work of this meeting. Are the dancers available? Has Beth brought the draft of the prayers?

Ordering the Service (20 minutes)

Typically in these moments, the group needs to finalize hymns and other music selections, finish writing and editing the prayers, determine the visual or media needs, and clarify any requirement for additional lay leadership (e.g., more communion servers or ushers).

Begin the discussion with the questions that will guide the work: What do we need to do to make space for the Spirit of God? Which options best reflect the message of God's Word this day? How can we hear and respond to the Word, preached and read?

Examining each element of the worship service in its context will help you craft a cohesive order, rather than a long sequence of actions (e.g., this hymn, then a prayer, then the anthem). Work through each portion of the service (Gathering, Hearing, Responding, Departing), considering its function in the whole. You need not begin with "Gathering." Sometimes, beginning in the middle of the order helps you see how to move into and out of various parts of the service. Look forward and backward. How does this hymn lead into the time of prayer? How does the congregational prayer reflect the metaphors of the hymn just sung?

There are multiple options within each section and a lot to consider. If you are stymied by questions or concerned that certain elements don't seem to fit ("This song seems more like a response than a preparation for the Word"), re-center the team members with the focus question: "What is God saying to us in the Word, and how can we respond?" Simple is best; we are making space for the Spirit, not overloading the order of worship just because we have good ideas.

The process itself is a bit like putting together a puzzle. The pieces that frame the service are solidly in place. The rhythms of gathering, hearing, responding, and departing are practices that we know, or are coming to know, by heart. Some of the responses (sung or spoken) continue from week to week. As in working on a puzzle, you may need to concentrate on one section for a while, then move to another and back again. As the picture emerges, you will be able to see where other pieces fit.

Seeing the Whole (15 minutes)

You have worked on sections; now look at the whole. Working from a bulletin template or the video script makes the flow of the worship service evident. The flow is the way elements move us through the service; it is the overall experiential shape of the liturgy. The intended flow is determined by the liturgical season, the text and theme, and pastoral considerations of the local context and circumstance. Are we entering with an exuberant hymn of praise and moving toward a more contemplative hearing of the Word that calls us to confession at the altar? Are we entering in a more subdued mood and leaving with energy and challenge for our witness in the world? Does the service move quickly or allow time for uninterrupted prayer at the altar? Do all the elements work together to make space for the presence of God and for the people's response to that Spirit?

As you work, the scribe fills in the draft of the worship bulletin, noting any remaining questions or concerns as well as particular tasks for the team on the day of the service. She will send the bulletin draft to the pastor and musician for any final editing. By the end of the meeting, the choices are in place. The beautiful ideas left over that will not fit into the service you are assembling for this day will find their place in another service.

Moving into the Space (15 minutes)

After you complete the ordering of the service, move into the worship space where you can discuss the logistics and see what is actually possible. You may have remembered that there is adequate room around the altar table, but when you consider how many servers will be involved, you realize that you need to move the table forward. If you gather the team in the worship space, you can refine the patterns of movement within the service. You may need to draw a diagram of a special procession, or check sightlines for multiple readers, or be sure the font is centrally located for the renewal of baptismal vows. Or, recalling the "new thing" in Ed's congregation, the Gospel procession, you may need to think in detail about how the Bible will be carried down the steps and into the center aisle. Other practical questions will arise: When the dancers are bringing in the bread and wine, will the ushers stand to the side or move back down the aisle? Can the children's choir move easily past the Chrismon tree to the chancel steps to sing?

Though not every service will have major logistical concerns, meeting in the space will make you more aware of those who will gather for worship. So move around in the space as you work together and talk about the service. If you are the pastor, sit in the congregational seats and imagine worship from another perspective.

SOME NOTES FROM AN "ORDERING" SESSION

The team members have worked together for several months and are familiar with the process and with each other's styles of conversation. They made some decisions quickly, like choosing the sung setting for communion and ending the service with a simple song of thanks. Other matters required more discussion. The following is their process of ordering the section "Hearing God's Word":

Preaching Text: Jeremiah 8:18–9:1. This will be the only text read.

THEME: Finding healing in the midst of crisis. (This service takes place in a busy time for the congregation when many decisions for the life of the community are pending.)

Discussion: The anthem is "Balm in Gilead." We discussed the choir's singing it before the text is read and then having the choir or the congregation sing the refrain again after the Scripture. Michael suggested that the reprise be an instrumental version. We agreed that it would provide a point of meditation before the sermon. He will ask Will to play alto sax (from the balcony).
Decision: Order for this section of the service: prayer for illumination; anthem, "Balm in Gilead"; reading of the Jeremiah text (Avis is the reader; she will give a powerful reading); "Balm in Gilead" refrain played by Will; sermon.

Summary

The ordering session focuses on the concrete choices for the assembly's participation in worship. The team's decisions are focused on this question: What are the essential elements needed in the service so that we might engage in hearing and responding to God's Word for us this day? In this session:

1. The team gathers for prayer.
2. Team members review the text, themes, and ideas, as well as any assignments from the planning session.
3. The team orders the service, making decisions about music, prayers, and other elements of worship.
4. The scribe completes the draft of the bulletin as the planners talk through the service, noting the flow of worship.
5. The team moves into the worship space to consider any logistical issues.
6. The scribe sends the completed bulletin to the pastor and music director for any final editing.

When you have put the details to rest, come together for a brief prayer. Remember those who will assemble for worship; picture them in their regular seats; listen to the sounds of singing and praying; see the hands that will receive bread and wine. Then pray that the preparation, planning, ordering, and rehearsal of the service might be a gracious offering for the Spirit of God, who will meet us as we gather for worship.

Chapter 6

Equipping Volunteer Leaders

The People in Ministry

Carol was in the sanctuary early on Sunday. She was scheduled to read the Scripture lessons, and she wanted to be ready. When she had first joined St. Elizabeth's Church, she noticed that the same three or four people always read the lessons. But a few months ago at the "ministries fair," which highlighted opportunities for service, she, along with several other new members, signed up to be a lay reader. They had attended a training session after worship and had been scheduled and given the Scripture texts for their assigned services. She moved to the lectern, read through the text one more time, and felt confident and prepared to offer her gift.

Though training volunteers for worship leadership may not be a direct responsibility of the planning team, well-trained leaders are such a crucial part of the service that we need to give some attention to equipping these lay ministers. Those currently involved in the worship ministries may be the ones who train the new volunteers. The chair of the usher board may recruit people for the ministry of hospitality. Altar guild members may teach those who prepare the sacramental elements and tend to the sacred space. In some congregations volunteers are carefully equipped with regular training events and refresher courses. In other congregations, this preparation is more ad hoc, even haphazard. The assumption seems to be that watching others in the roles is training enough.

The introduction of a planning model that expands congregational participation requires new attention to recruiting, training, and scheduling lay ministers for service. As the team is organizing and putting the service into form, its scope is expanding to include those other ministers: ushers, greeters, communion servers, readers, cantors, acolytes, bread bakers, visual designers. The planning team members will share their enthusiasm for the upcoming services, and more volunteers will respond. The volunteers want to do well—they want to read clearly, serve communion with confidence, and meet those who enter with genuine welcome. They are the ones who will assist the gathered assembly in making worship come alive. The best ideas and the most detailed ordering will fall flat if the needed leadership is not prepared and in place. Who are these people and how are they equipped for ministry?

Defining the Ministries

As you prepare to recruit and train lay ministers for the liturgy, you will find it helpful to develop a set of job descriptions, or "customaries," to assist in defining the various liturgical ministries in your congregation. As we use the term, a *customary* is an outline of the liturgical practice in a particular context that also reflects historic and denominational practice. It is the ordered "way we do it here." Brief examples of customaries are listed in Appendix D.

As the coordinators of these ministries work with the pastor on the guidelines, questions will arise, such as "Why do we do this?" and "What does this action signify?" This may be a good time to revisit the roles and functions of the lay ministers and refine some of the not-so-well-done performance practices, such as the haphazard lighting of the altar candles or the need for better training of the lay deacons to assist at the table. You may need to revise time-honored routines in light of this new planning process. A detailed and up-to-date customary can serve as a checklist for the duties and a guideline for evaluating both the ministry and the minister. You will want to develop definitions and instructions that are specific to your congregation. The following list defines some liturgical ministries that are present in many congregations. You will add others.

Communion servers assist as lay ministers at the communion feast. Their quiet gestures of respect for the sacrament and those communing assure all a welcome place at the table.

Readers or liturgists are lay ministers of the Word. They read the Scripture texts and lead the people in prayer. Their clear and articulate reading conveys the importance of the living Word of God.

Altar guild members or sacristans are ministers of preparation—of the communion elements, the altar, and the pulpit area specifically, and of the worship space generally. This ministry is essential for the assembly's reverence of Word and Sacrament.

Greeters and ushers are ministers of hospitality whose gestures of greeting and words of grace assure a welcome to all who enter. Their gentle directions guide the assembly as the people offer their gifts or come to receive the sacraments.

Cantors or song leaders are the ministers of song. Their confident gestures and clear directions enable the people's song in worship.

Acolytes are those who lead the procession into the sanctuary bearing the Light of Christ. They also serve as torchbearers, or carry the Word into the midst of the assembly for the reading of the Gospel, and assist the pastor as directed in the service.

Recruiting

Most congregations need and welcome new volunteers for liturgical ministries. Read any newsletter or bulletin; the door is usually open. However, a general, ongoing invitation or call for ushers or readers or communion servers or choir members often is read as a casual announcement rather than a call to an essential ministry in the worship life of the parish. Few may volunteer. Any of the following ideas may bring better results.

A Personal Invitation

Recall some of the stories in the earlier chapters of this book. Jeff was personally asked to serve on the planning team by his pastor, Margaret. In Matt's new congregation, members are invited to serve as planners for a service so that they can learn more about worship practices. If you, as a leader or pastor, notice people with gifts for specific lay ministries—a person who speaks particularly well in public, who has gifts of hospitality, or whose skills at flower arranging or baking are known—invite them with a note or phone call or face to face. Connect them with the coordinator of the appropriate ministries. Affirm their gifts for service, and assure them that they will be equipped for their task.

A Detailed Presentation of the Ministry

A majority of Christian congregations give time in the worship service for presentations on financial stewardship or mission trips. Why not a brief presentation on the work of lay ministers in the liturgy? Knowing the specifics of a ministry heightens people's awareness of its importance as they witness the work of these ministers in worship. For example, most young people sign up to serve as acolytes because they have watched others in the role and want to take part in it. Remember Carol at the beginning of this chapter, who noticed the lay readers and was drawn to that ministry.

A "Ministries Fair"

Many congregations have an annual "ministries fair" at which the various opportunities for service within the church and in the world are highlighted. People who work with local missions, youth ministries, children's concerns, prison ministries, or help for the homeless set up information tables, answer questions, and engage in conversation. If your parish hosts such an event, be sure that there is also a table for "Serving in Liturgy" that offers helpful, colorful brochures with "tear-offs" for expressing interest or signing up. Invite the most knowledgeable and enthusiastic leaders to serve as hosts for the table.

Online Recruiting

If you have a page on your church's website for "volunteers," be sure that people can volunteer to serve in worship. Post photos of the lay ministers in their various liturgical roles; include brief testimonies or video clips with statements from current volunteers. Be sure any online applications are user-friendly.

Follow Up

Whatever venues or methods of recruitment your church adopts, be sure that those who volunteer know:

1. When they will be contacted and scheduled for training or orientation to their ministry. Ideally, they should receive a call, note, or e-mail within a week of signing up, confirming their interest and inviting them to a training session.
2. How often they will serve in this capacity. Every week? Once a month?
3. The length of their term of service: One season? One year?
4. When they will receive the schedule for their service.

Training

Congregants who volunteer their gifts of time and talent should expect to be prepared for their ministry. They should be trained for the role and given all the information they need before the service. And those who recruit, train, and schedule the volunteers need to plan far enough ahead to avoid last-minute requests. "Can you just read the first lesson today? It's marked in the Bible on the pulpit desk." "Just reading" is a dismissal of the importance of both the reader and the biblical text. An unrehearsed reading risks mispronounced words and casual articulation. Both the reader and the congregation will be anxious if the reader stumbles, and the Word will not be given full attention. Occasionally a last-minute change in readers is necessary, but if this is the norm, why would one volunteer?

Members of the congregation will usually respond positively to an invitation for service that includes training to equip them for better service. In our context, a seminary in which people are training for ministry and expected to speak and read aloud every day, those who sign up for worship leadership are required to come for a brief orientation to practice reading prayers and scriptural texts in the worship space. We do not assume that they will know the feel of the wobbly step up to the pulpit, the sound of their voice through the microphone, or that, on the spot, they will know the pronunciation of every complex biblical name. Likewise, those who serve at the table with the presider and the deacon are scheduled for a brief orientation.

You may wish to hold orientation or training sessions as an extension of the regular Sunday gathering. Having just participated in worship, and having seen others in the roles, new volunteers are attentive to the specifics of the liturgical actions and are ready to learn. Provide a simple lunch for all the liturgical volunteers. The pastor or coordinator of worship ministries should briefly lead the gathered volunteers through the worship service with emphasis on the roles of the lay ministers. Then, divide into various groups—acolytes, readers, ushers, communion servers, lay deacons, or others particular to your congregation—for specific and detailed training by the coordinator of each of these ministries.

Scheduling Volunteers

Having been trained, volunteers are ready for service. It is essential that those who have signed up and have been trained then be scheduled. Even if their date of service is a few months off, their gift is already recognized and accepted. Depending on the size of the congregation, you may have a coordinator who schedules each of the liturgical ministries, or two people may make all the assignments.

Most congregations find it advantageous to schedule the lay leaders for several months, or for a season, at a time. A published spreadsheet or chart in the church's newsletter or on an internal webpage listing the lay ministers for the various services serves as a reminder to those volunteers and allows them to swap dates if they have a conflict. Working from a spreadsheet also ensures that the coordinators do not assign the same people to multiple duties on any one day. As they are preparing and ordering the upcoming worship, the planning team members know who is assigned to the various roles. If a particular service, such as a Service of Nine Lessons and Carols at Christmas, needs additional readers, the planners can contact the coordinator of that ministry and know that trained readers will be assigned. Or if the planners anticipate a special procession for All Saints Sunday, they can confer in advance with the acolyte coordinator or the leader of the usher team for the day. Scheduling the liturgical leaders far enough in advance allows for smooth planning and implementation of the worship service, and encourages good communication among all the parties.

Blessing and Recognition of Lay Volunteers

Bless and dedicate these ministers to their service in the liturgy. Most denominational books of worship have brief rituals to commission volunteers and lay leaders. And when their time of service is completed, recognize and give thanks for their ministry. The blessings and gestures of appreciation can be a part of the worship service, a ritual that often comes at the beginning or end of the school year.

The liturgical volunteers are the ones who make the planning and ordering come alive; they are the ones who lead through gestures of hospitality, through the animation of songs, in the clear and careful reading of Scripture and prayers, in the preparation and decoration of the space, in the baking of bread and the serving of consecrated elements. These representatives embody the liturgy, the work of all the people.

The pastor's own ministry will be strengthened by the lay ministers who serve alongside. Mollie, the associate pastor at a large urban church, commented after her congregation had begun to use the POWR model:

> I am now relying more heavily on laypeople to assist me in designing worship and in recruiting individuals to participate in worship. I also have worked to train volunteers more thoroughly. I realized that we had not been referring to their work as "ministry" and that I needed to prayerfully direct people according to their gifts into specific worship ministries. For example, the greeters were trained with much more emphasis on Christian hospitality this year. I encouraged them to be more sensitive to visitors—and to what barriers guests may have had to overcome to attend our services or to enter the building.

The defined liturgical ministries carry with them an expectation for excellence and accountability. As lay ministers are equipped for service, they acquire confidence in fulfilling their liturgical responsibilities. The people are empowered for leadership; the pastor is freed to focus on the pastoral-priestly-prophetic role in worship. The liturgy becomes the work of all who gather. Together the congregation is fully engaged in the worship of God.

Chapter 7

Worship

The Work of All the People

It is ten minutes before the scheduled worship at St. John Church. In the choir room, the singers are rehearsing a difficult rhythm with the conga player one last time before they move into the sanctuary. In the chancel area, two teenage guitar players and a flutist are tuning up to prepare for accompanying the psalm of the day. The organist and the pianist are conferring on tempos for the opening voluntary. Jerry has just finished a sound check with the drama group, which will be enacting the Gospel lesson. In the vestibule, the ushers are putting the wet umbrellas in the corner, directing visiting families to the nursery, and handing out the bulletins. The children from the fourth-grade Sunday school class are receiving the bags of canned goods that people are bringing for the food pantry. The acolytes are robed and ready, candle-lighting tapers in hand. The communion elements are on a side table in the vestibule, with freshly baked bread (still warm) from John and Nancy. In her office, Ann puts on her robe and stole and listens to the sounds and imagines the faces of those who are gathering—coming from the parking lot or from Christian education classes, greeting friends, welcoming visitors. She thinks of all who will lead the worship on this day. She prays with the deacon and picks up her hymnal, and they move toward the sanctuary.

Whether the congregation meets in a sanctuary, a fellowship hall, a gym, or a school cafeteria, the moments before the service are a time of expectation. The final preparation, the rituals of greeting and gathering, and the gestures and words of welcome are the embodied signs that the assembly's work is beginning. What are the indications that a congregation is participating in richer worship? What is the evidence that the people are maturing in their spiritual journeys? Let's take a closer look at the gathered assembly.

Signs of Renewal

Some features of a richer liturgy will stand out. In the best times of worship, all those assembled are fully engaged in the praise of God. The prayers and the singing are heartfelt; the gestures and movement are meaningful. The whole service moves along in one seamless motion. There are no jarring disruptions or ill-prepared transitions from one element of the service to another. Regular worshipers know the *ordo* in this place, and their practiced participation encourages those who are visiting.

Attention to Detail

As the worship unfolds, attention to detail becomes noticeable. Careful conversation among planners, pastor, and musicians in all the preparatory stages enables the service to flow smoothly. The organist knows that the procession for a festival day will include more people, and she is prepared with an interlude and modulation before the final stanza of the hymn. The other musicians are ready to make transitions from one song to another to lead into the time of prayer. The dancers and musicians have conferred and rehearsed together, so the final doxological stanza of the offertory hymn will begin as the dancers place the gifts on the altar.

Other ministries will show the same conscientious preparation. The liturgists and readers have received training; they lead the prayers and read the Scripture lessons with clarity and confidence. The altar guild has expanded to include the flower guild, and the chancel area is beautifully dressed. In worship spaces that use video projection, the altar designs and the artwork on the screens are coordinated to enhance the impact of symbol and color. The projected text is easily read and is not jarring or intrusive. The service bulletin is user-friendly. In a gesture of welcome to neighbor and stranger, the bulletin includes texts for the Lord's Prayer and other ritual words and actions that may not be familiar to all. Signs direct visitors to various areas of the building, and greeters are stationed at every entrance.

Multiple Leaders

Preparing and integrating more volunteers into leadership will be smooth, now that training and scheduling have been put in place. As more people are involved in planning and leading, the conversation about worship expands. Each of these members has circles of friends and contacts, and areas of influence. The word gets out. "Something is happening at church, and you will want to be involved." You will see new faces in leadership. Some of the familiar faces will be freed to fill other roles, and imagine new ministries—or to take a break from long years of service.

The planning team members themselves are not necessarily the leaders in worship; however, they have the concept of the whole service in mind. They have walked through the order, felt the flow of the service, imagined the movement in the space, and confirmed that all is ready. Because they are not the "up-front" leaders, the team members can work on the details around the edges of the service or behind the scenes. One of them may gather with the communion servers to answer any last-minute questions. Another may check to see that the dancers are ready for the procession. Their presence reassures other leaders and relieves the pastor of concern for the minutiae.

We were working to involve the youth in more worship ministries and were excited when six high-school students volunteered to be ushers. This could have been one more team for the regular Sunday rotation of passing out the bulletins and collecting the offering. But in conversation, the young people suggested an expansion of the ministry of hospitality to include assistance to families with young children. These new ushers now meet the families at the door nearest the children's wing. They assist in getting the children to nursery or Sunday school classes. The youth are friendly faces and helping hands for these hurried parents.

—PAUL, CHAIR OF THE USHER BOARD

When the planning team includes people of varying ages, abilities, and life-stages, the leadership in worship likely will reflect that. At St. John Church, one member of the planning team is the mother of one of the active and eager fourth-graders who receive the canned goods that worshipers bring with them to church. When the planners discussed bringing the food to the altar as part of the offertory procession, they realized that assigning this task to the fourth-graders was a perfect fit. The children's enthusiasm for the task has become contagious; the amount of food collected has increased, and the children are involved in meaningful work.

One member of the planning team has a severe hearing impairment. His leadership has significantly raised awareness of hospitality to those with particular needs and abilities. As a result, the church has modified the choir area to welcome a woman in a wheelchair, and among the regular liturgists is a man whose guide dog sits beside him. A line in the bulletin informs worshipers, "Rows 3 and 5 in the pews on the right are equipped with assisted listening devices and reserved for those who need them to hear the service more clearly."

In another instance, an older member of the planning team mentioned the difficulty some members experience attending worship in the winter months and their desire to receive Holy Communion more often than is possible with only the pastor's occasional visits. Now, thanks to the lay ministers who visit and bring the consecrated elements, members unable to leave their homes are part of the gathered congregation. These ministers don't just take the elements after the service but receive the blessing of the whole assembly before they leave: "We send you forth bearing these gifts . . . for we who are many are one Body, for we are all one in Christ."[1] Through this action, the table is extended beyond the walls of the building.

Multiple Expressions

I had always worked with the musicians to coordinate the sermon and the musical elements of worship, but since we have formed a planning team, the whole service ties together. We have a particularly talented group of women who prepare visual arrangements in front of the altar each week to interpret the preaching text. I had no idea how this would enhance my own preaching, but the conversation around the text and their visual designs make the sermon come alive. We have included photos of these designs on our website, and seeing these designs in the sanctuary and online has attracted more people into our visual arts ministry.

—SCOTT, PASTOR

As the conversational model and the discussion questions that guide the process become a part of the congregation's vocabulary and thinking, additional sensory expressions will be suggested in the planning and will be included in the service. The language developed in the planning meetings to describe the look, feel, and sound of the texts carries into the worship space with texture and color in paraments and processional banners, in seasonal flowers or plants, in visual designs at the entrance or around the altar. The sounds and actions of the biblical narrative find expression in drama or song, in video or print that brings the text to life. Members of the congregation will engage the themes of the day in multiple ways—visually, aurally, tactilely—and the message of the sermon will be heightened as the people respond to the Word through these avenues. In addition to multistanza hymns, the congregation is singing more short songs and choruses. Easily learned, these songs are especially meaningful to those who long for both meditation and spontaneity. The songs also invite strong participation by children and the intellectually challenged; there are not a lot of words to read from the book or screen. At St. John Church, the freshly baked communion bread offers an immediate invitation to the feast, a sign of nourishment for the body and spirit, a feeling of comfort and "home." The visible sign of children bringing the offering of food gives witness to the congregation's ministry in the world.

The styles of prayer are expanding, too. In one service, the congregation may be led by the pastor's extemporaneous prayer, and may also participate in brief prayers spoken aloud by the whole congregation, a prayer of blessing sung in Chinese by the choir, and prayers for the world written and led by the junior-high youth. The musicians may lead the people in chanting a psalm, or in singing the Lord's Prayer. Many people are finding voice and a language of expression.

Many Gifts

> People have been shaped in positive ways. One woman who participated in the planning meetings volunteered to serve communion for that week. She was so excited that she invited her parents to attend. She had never had that sort of opportunity. Our church is full of stories of people finding a place where they can give expression to their stories and to a faith that is beginning to shape those stories.
>
> —NATE, PASTOR

As the communion elements, the gifts of money, and the cans of food for the hungry are brought forward in the offertory procession, it is clear that this offering is more than tangible gifts. The worshipers are offering themselves—their time and talents and lives. These are offerings of study and conversation; of phone calls, e-mails, and rehearsals; of gardening and sewing and baking; of raking, cleaning, and straightening up; of child care and the mentoring of youth. The people are becoming more aware that all the preparations and the work of their hands are given as part of their ongoing life in Christ in the company of each other. The gathering and hearing, feasting and departing are expressed in the Isaac Watts text "O may thy house be my abode, and all my work be praise."[2] This is the liturgy, the work of all the gathered people.

Chapter 8

Reflecting

A Conversation after Worship

After the worship service Mark often overheard such comments as "Wasn't the music just great this morning?" and "Did you see the detailed work on those beautiful new banners?" People met him at the door and said, "That was a fine sermon, Pastor." Or sometimes they mentioned that the organ was too loud or that the sound system was faulty. Mark knew that these expressions of preference or dislike and the reports of needed repairs, while valid, did not represent a considered reflection on the worship service. He longed for a conversation that reflected deeply on the people's participation in the liturgy and on the many ways they were being formed in faith.

The reflection that Mark desires for his congregation, and that this chapter discusses, is an engagement in what Gordon Lathrop calls "secondary liturgical theology." He defines the term as "discourse that attempts to find words for the experience of the liturgy and to illuminate its structure, intending to enable a more profound participation . . . by the members of the assembly."[1] The reflection session in the conversational model is such discourse. We will step back from the work of worshiping to consider what we did and what it meant. In reflecting on the meaning of the worship service, we are preparing to reenter the liturgy, ready to immerse ourselves in it again.

The guided reflection happens soon after the service. In some congregations the planners meet over lunch immediately after worship. The memories are clear, and the songs are still echoing in the soul. Congregations that have a Sunday-evening Bible study may use a bit of this time to reflect on the morning worship. You may find that meeting a few days after the worship service allows a more objective vantage. It often takes time for the memories to settle, to take shape in the mind and heart. A pastor notes, "Having a few days to process on their own helps people come prepared to the group meetings. The team members come with notes and are able to express themselves a lot more succinctly." In larger congregations, the staff may reflect on the service at its weekly meeting. However, the staff reflection does not take the place of a conversation involving the whole team. Some teams, as noted in chapter 3, reflect on previous services as they meet for their next planning session.

Leading the Conversation

Most people will be familiar with reflection processes that essentially evaluate what "worked" or what was "effective." Such reflection centers on our responsibilities in worship. Someone begins the conversation by recalling the clumsy attempts to light the new wicks on the altar candles. Another person in the circle comments on the fumbled lines in the dramatic reading. These "glaring errors" negatively affected worship for them. Slip-ups like these may even be seen as "failures"—of our efforts or of the planning process itself. The members of a planning team have a lot invested in the preparation for the service, and they will want to fix the mistakes (or "never do *that* again"). This is a natural reaction; we want our own part in the praise of God to be a worthy offering.

The conversational model does not overlook those concerns but puts them in a different perspective. We need to consider whether our worship reflected the themes of the biblical text and the intentions of the planners. We want to know whether, over time, the congregation is being renewed and strengthened in faith and in service. However, the first questions that guide the reflection flow from the belief that it is God's action in worship that invites our response. In this session, we center on the overarching question: "How were we called as God's people, met and confronted by the risen Christ, and sent into the world through the power of the Holy Spirit?" This is a trinitarian model for reflecting on God's presence and power in our gathering.

> The reflection session causes us to pay more attention to worship and why things happen the way they do, and has given us permission to be freer and more creative in our worship. We know that God is working in our planning, and meets us in the sanctuary to bless our efforts. This change in attitude is affecting the rest of the congregation. People are beginning to volunteer their own artistic gifts. They are starting to see worship as our offering.
>
> —AUDREY, PLANNING TEAM MEMBER

The Reflection Process

As the team gathers, the leader should see that each person has a service bulletin or the script of the service. The scribe will again take notes. Appedix E is a leader's guide for the reflecting process.

Gather (5 minutes)

Come together with a centering silence and a brief prayer. Especially if the reflection closely follows the worship service, the remembered sound of water being poured, the sight of dancers twirling, the touch of hands in greeting, and the taste of the bread will all be sharp in the minds of the team members. Sit for a moment. Be still and be thankful.

Let us pray:
O God, you have gone before us in all our work,
in our time of planning and preparing to worship you,
in all the rehearsing and reading, in the baking of bread,
the arranging of flowers.
You met us as we gathered for worship;
you spoke in song and silence, in Word and meal,
in our gathering and departing.
Be with us now in this time of reflecting
that we might remember your presence with us always.
All praise to you, God, Three in One. Amen.

Reflect on the Service (15-20 minutes)

If you are reflecting on an entire season, or on the introduction of new elements into the service, you may need an extended time of reflection. The questions below can guide the discussion. You will refine these and think of others.

The first set of questions. The first part of the reflection session recalls God's presence and action in the time of worship. The focus question is this: In our worship how did we encounter the faithful work of God, the presence of the risen Christ, and the life-giving power of the Holy Spirit?

1. What words would you use to describe this time of worship?
2. How did you perceive the Spirit of God moving among us? What did you see, hear, taste, smell, and touch?
3. In what ways did you hear the Good News of Christ? What made the Word of God come alive?
4. How was the congregation challenged or strengthened in this time of worship?
5. Were there elements of surprise? If so, what were they?
6. In what ways were the people attentive and participating?
7. How is our congregation growing closer to God and how are congregants growing closer to one another through worship?
8. How are we being equipped to be the body of Christ in the world?

These are questions for discussion, not to be answered with a simple yes or no. They engage the team in faith-filled speech, a language that speaks about our relationship with God and our encounter with God in worship. By using questions like this in leading the conversation, you will teach this language. Most people default to the language of preference in reflection: "I liked the sermon." "I didn't like the anthem." People need—and our experience shows they will welcome—a larger vocabulary to describe what happens to them in worship.

The second set of questions. The next part of the reflection centers on our own work and offering: How were we hospitable to the neighbor and welcoming of the stranger?

1. In what ways did we offer hospitality to all? What people felt invited into this service? Who may have felt excluded? Were spoken and printed directions clear? In what ways did we include the children, the aged, those with special needs, and the stranger?
2. Did all the elements of the service (hymns and songs, prayer words and postures, visual designs, and other sensory experiences) support the message of the scriptural texts?
3. How did our preparation enable the work of all the people, the liturgy? In what ways was it a hindrance?
4. Did the service flow smoothly and coherently?
5. Were the leaders effectively equipped? Readers? Servers? Ushers? Others? Were there any impediments to their leadership in this service? What improvements should we make?
6. Was the technology helpful? Was the sound clear? Was the lighting adequate? Was the video engaging and relevant, not distracting? Were the print materials easy to read?
7. Did we use the space wisely? Could people (processions, dancers, drama participants, leaders) get where they needed to go? Were the visual elements easily seen and understood?
8. What other details are worth noting?

This discussion deals primarily with the large issue of hospitality, of welcoming God's Spirit and God's people. One of the leadership responsibilities in this session is helping the team members to see that all their preparation—everything they do to get ready for worship—is a grace-filled act of ministry, offered to God.

Our conversation about hospitality has become a theological reflection about what it means to welcome others in the name of Christ. It has been especially transformative in the lead usher's seeing herself as a worship leader more than a "volunteer."

—Beth, pastor of an older congregation

Concluding the Session (5 minutes)

Review the comments and reflections. As you do, note:

1. Which practices were valuable? ("We can do this again.") The team may have introduced small but significant changes or elements to the worship service. The congregation has responded in positive ways. Make note, and do this again. "Moving the altar table closer to the people really made everyone welcome. People could see, and they paid closer attention, especially the children." "Singing the psalm as a prayer was a powerful expression of those ancient words." "People loved singing the song from Zimbabwe!"
2. Which items need consideration? ("We will pay attention to this.") As you evaluate, in a systematic way or informally in planning sessions or staff meetings, it may become apparent that certain practices or habits need some reevaluation, or over time you may need to pay attention to the shape or tone of the worship services. "Lately most of the hymns are about God as majestic and powerful. We need to balance those with some songs about God's presence on our journey." "We need to rehearse the readers with microphones and have each do a sound check."
3. Which concerns can be corrected or improved with a phone call or an e-mail? ("We will assign a team member to do this now.") Some of the practical points that receive mention in the reflection time can be noted and attended to on the spot. Assign this "action item" to a team member. "More people are requesting large-print bulletins." "The ushers need to have umbrellas ready for rainy days." "The flower arrangements were spectacular! The new flower guild is really contributing to the worship. Let's be sure to send Alice a note."
4. Which points need more thoughtful discussion? ("Let's schedule a time for a longer conversation about this.") In the course of the reflection, some larger concerns may arise that call for an extended conversation with the pastoral leadership, or even with the church's governing body. Some concerns may

> involve making major changes in the order of worship, or addressing some fundamental issues of hospitality. "People are commenting about the jerkiness between parts of the service, especially with the collection of the offering." "Having the announcements just before the opening hymn interrupts the mood of reverence." "You know, just getting into our church building requires coming up several stairs, which is prohibitive for people who use walkers or wheelchairs. As part of our ministry of hospitality, we need to think about making our space more accessible."

The scribe will send the notes around to the team and the pastor and music director. If this is the end of a season, or of a term of service, the scribe may send the notes to the incoming team for reference or follow-up on any major issues or long-term concerns. The facilitator should dismiss the group with a blessing and thanks for their ministry and service.

A planning team reports: Our team was surprised as we heard these responses in the reflection session:

How did you feel the Spirit of God moving among us?

"In the call and response between the balconies as we read the psalm that told of God's mighty deeds. It was expansive!"

"The sounds of the chant stirred me (even though it is probably the furthest from my music/worship comfort zone)."

"In the reading, I could taste the manna and quail! What if we'd had real food on the altar?"

What adjectives would you use to describe this service?

"Celebratory."

"Fully embodied, powerful."

"Silent."

"Satisfying."

We wondered how this could be! Weren't there some contradictions in these responses? Then we realized that all the statements were apt descriptions of the service. People of all four spiritual types (head spirituality, heart spirituality, mystic spirituality, and kingdom spirituality) had found a place and had responded to the worship service in varied ways. It was a wonderful moment of discovering our diversity and oneness in Christ.

Summary

In the reflection session the people recall what happened in worship, how God's actions and our response strengthened us for service and brought us into closer relationship with Christ.

1. The team gathers with thanks for God's presence.
2. Team members reflect on the service, beginning with God's presence and action in worship and moving through the logistical and practical aspects of the service.
3. They organize the notes—items needing immediate attention and those with long-term implications.
4. They hand the reflection notes to the next team, or prepare to begin the planning process again.

The End Is the Beginning

In reflection we are seeing over time:

1. More people have leadership roles and are engaged in worship.
2. Music is well thought out and better led.
3. More voices are being heard in worship.
4. There is increased variety in proclamation of the word, prayer, and response.

—MATT, PASTOR OF AN URBAN CONGREGATION

Insights from the reflection sessions lead back into planning for the next services or season. The reflection is not the end; it actually begins the process. But as the planning begins again, the team members themselves will have grown. The enriched vocabulary of the conversations, the increased capacity for discussion, and the depth of curiosity about biblical texts are evidence of this spiritual maturity.

> Through our work of planning, we have increased our understanding of the liturgy and have learned to recognize traditional liturgical elements in contemporary variations. This knowledge was important in our conservative, rural congregation. The congregation accepted "new" ways of worshiping because worship services were planned by trusted laypersons. We all gained a feeling of ownership, which strengthened our church community. When the pastor moved on, our committee remained and helped the new pastor settle in to our congregation.
>
> —CAROLYN, PLANNING TEAM MEMBER

At certain times—the end of the season, as a team completes a term of service, as planning begins for a new year—the planning team will want to spend a significant portion of the hour reflecting on worship services over a longer time period. Team members can begin to articulate and celebrate the deeper spiritual life into which the congregation is being formed and led, and the increased love of God and neighbor that is evident. The team can point to ways in which the church is providing avenues of welcome for a diversity of people. The perspective from this longer vantage point of remembrance and reflection will provide insights into the ongoing encounter with God, who is doing a new thing in your midst.

Chapter 9

Musicians

Leading the People in Song

Alice is the part-time choir director and organist at a church of about one hundred members. The adult choir, with six to fifteen members depending on the season, rehearses on Thursdays before the evening Bible study. The choir leads the hymns and service music and, about once a month, sings an anthem. Across town, Steve, a full-time minister of music, directs a program involving six graded children's choirs, three handbell choirs, a praise band, and an adult choir of fifty-five members. This highly organized ministry provides anthems or special music for every worship service of the year. In another congregation Robert serves with a team of musicians, each responsible for music on a different Sunday of the month. He directs the senior choir, which sings on the second Sunday and is accompanied by organ and piano. The singers rehearse on two successive Wednesdays before the Sunday they will sing.

The work of these musicians is diverse in structure, content, and scheduling. And yet all three are a part of the same ministry. Throughout this book and in various congregations a variety of terms are used to designate the leader of the congregation's music: music director, music leader, choir director, praise-band leader, organist/pianist, choirmaster. If you are a musician at your church, no matter your title, your primary work is to encourage and lead the congregation's praise and sung prayer. In this capacity you are the "pastoral musician." You are also a teacher of music and poetry, an interpreter of biblical texts, a student of your musical craft, and a minister of the gospel of Jesus Christ. Working in partnership with the pastor, the planning team, choirs, and other musicians, you will exercise all these facets of your vocation in the planning, ordering, and reflective conversations.

Working in Partnership

Many books have been written about the working relationships among pastors, musicians, and choirs, usually as a response to the difficulties encountered (or expected). The POWR model presumes a partnership between the leaders of sermon and song, a connection between the proclamation of the Word and the people's response. Before putting this model into practice, you should be in conversation with the pastor and key leaders to decide what your role in the process will be. Any agreements should support your primary ministry: enabling the worshiping assembly's song.

We have already given attention to the variety of spiritual types and to people's needs for different worship patterns and styles. All those in pastoral roles should participate in the worship survey (appendix A) and the spiritual type inventory (outlined in chapter 3) along with members of the congregation. In looking at the responses to both, you will see (and celebrate) differences in the musicians' and pastors' personalities and preferences.

The conversational model of planning provides ways to speak to one another with respect and appreciation across these differences and to take advantage of your unique roles and talents. Working together and engaging the questions in each step of the planning model, you can move beyond individual claims and past territorial ways of thinking. So, for example, when questions of worship style arise, the conversational model avoids divisive clichéd terms and helps to focus the discussion on such questions as "What is God saying to us (to this congregation) and how shall we respond?" and "What expressions and practices will form us more deeply into the likeness of Christ?" The questions guide pastors and musicians into a conversational arena that embraces all gifts. The model presupposes that both pastors and musicians are in ministry and that the shared pastoral task of caring for the people, and the people's worship, is fundamental.

The Pastoral Musician and the POWR Process

The pastoral musician (music leader, minister, director, or cantor) is integral to the success of the conversational process and, like the pastor, will need to prepare for the planning meetings. Just as the preaching minister will have studied the biblical texts and begun to uncover themes for the sermons prior to the planning sessions, the pastoral musician will have begun to lay out musical elements for the seasons.

Many musicians spend significant time in the less hectic summer months reading through hymns and songs and music for choirs, studying the lectionary or preaching texts, and ordering music for the upcoming year. You will have thought about the major festivals of the church year and will have selected some anthems or keyboard music. Depending on the program at your church, many of these decisions will be in place before the planning team meets for the season or for particular services. On the other hand, you may be a volunteer or part-time music director, or you may have responsibilities as a member of the music team. You may choose anthems or service music a week or two before a service, when you have ascertained which members of the choir will be present. Or the rhythm of your work may lie somewhere between these two examples. So, whether planning several months ahead or only a few weeks out, how does the musician come to the planning meeting ready to "brainstorm"?

Joining the Conversation

In the planning meeting, as team members are describing the images they hear and see in the biblical text, the musician may be recalling the words and music of hymns or songs. The musician's liturgical language and vocabulary tend to be drawn from memorable musical and lyrical phrases. When others in the circle are articulating the "feel" of the preaching text, you may be thumbing through the several songbooks you have brought with you, taking notes as you listen to the conversation. Your knowledge of a wide spectrum of hymns and songs, of choruses, of service music and sung responses will help keep the conversation moving as you offer suggestions or provide options.

If you come to the meeting with most of the anthems or special music selected, these prior decisions can enrich the conversation. For example, you may have chosen a setting of "Shall We Gather at the River" for All Saints services. As the team members hear the assigned reading from the book of Revelation and imagine the vivid scenes in both the biblical text and the anthem, someone might say, "All this makes me think of baptism and the sound of water poured into the font." And another person might say, "Could we move the font to the center of the chancel to remind us of all those saints who were baptized in this place?" In this instance, the musical selections spawn a discussion about ways the service could involve all the senses.

> As the planning team members were randomly thumbing through the hymnal, it occurred to me that these folks had sung many of the hymns and songs but were unfamiliar with the organization of the book or how to find what they were searching for. I suggested we spend a few minutes learning about the indexes and the structure of the contents. This proposal generated a slew of questions and some "aha!" moments of discovery. The team members began eagerly exploring the hymnal and its contents. Since then, all the planners have come to the meetings with new suggestions and ideas for congregational songs and hymns.
>
> —CAROL, MUSIC DIRECTOR OF A MIDSIZE CONGREGATION

Worship planners new to their task may not express many ideas for musical elements in the service, because they consider the musician the "expert" and turn to you for ideas. But as you affirm their ideas and seize opportunities to teach and encourage the members of the team, you will help make the planning meeting an inviting circle in which to wonder, imagine, and ask questions.

You and the pastor will have opportunity to teach about the liturgy and the function of music in each part of the service. As you discuss the themes for the day and the ways in which the congregation prepares for or responds to the hearing of the Word, the team members will gain insight into the rhythms of the worship service. As members rotate off the team, you will receive a new group of people eager to learn and put into practice their knowledge of music in the liturgy.

Build on the curiosity of the group. Take advantage of the suggestions for familiar hymns, and see what other songs appear on nearby pages of the hymnal. Play through the tunes to help connect the mood of the biblical text with the music the congregation might sing. Read the texts of the hymns suggested in the brainstorming session. Not every text need be sung. A hymn stanza might be read aloud as a prayer or printed in the bulletin to focus the meditation of worshipers as they gather. The pastor might decide to incorporate phrases of a hymn in the pastoral prayer, or the congregation might sing a phrase of a hymn in response to petitions. One pastor said, "The time spent reading the hymn texts aloud was probably one of the high points of the planning process for me. By choosing songs based on the biblical theme, we were able to add to the cohesiveness of the service."

Ordering

The final selection of hymns and songs and service music is usually a part of the ordering conversation. You may be participating in this session in person, or another musician may be representing your ministry. As we noted in chapter 3, some congregations complete the ordering (and the final selection of hymns and songs) as a part of regular staff meetings. You can also guide the choice or placement of the hymns through e-mail notes, reminding the planners of the character of a particular text and tune. ("Consider using the tune "Hyfrydol" as the opening hymn and the song 'We Say Yes' as a response to the sermon.")

One congregation, looking for ways to include as many familiar carols as possible on Christmas Eve, used the third stanza of "O Little Town of Bethlehem" as the response to the breaking of the bread (the fraction) in Holy Communion: "How silently, how silently the wondrous gift is given . . ." Ideas like this will spring up in the conversation when you listen attentively and with a pastoral ear to the diverse voices on the planning team.

At other times, the suggestions may confuse or irritate you. You may be thinking, "That hymn has nothing to do with the season" or "Not again! Why not something new?" Listen; take another look. Perhaps the third stanza is exactly the needed call to prayer for that day. If you are wrestling with the suggestion that the congregation sing "Amazing Grace" one more Sunday, think about the possibilities for new accompaniment, or a solo voice from the distance, or the impact of the final stanza's affirmation, "When we've been there ten thousand years . . . ," sung as an end to the feast at the table.

A verbatim from a planning team in a mid-sized congregation illustrates the give-and-take that can enliven the choice of music.

Mark, the pianist and choir director: After our planning session I kept looking through the hymnals in my library to find a song about healing that would be just right for the Gospel lesson [Jesus's healing the man with an unclean spirit, Luke 4:31–37]. Listen. *[He plays and sings "Healer of Our Every Ill" by Marty Haugen.]* Could we sing it before or after the sermon?

Sharon, the pastor: Does this song lead us into hearing the Gospel, or do we need to have heard the sermon before we can sing it with understanding?

Mark: Listen to the refrain again:

Healer of our every ill, light of each tomorrow,
give us peace beyond our fear, and hope beyond our sorrow.[1]

Martha, lay member: It's really a prayer, isn't it? Maybe we could sing it before the prayers of the people. We have some folks in our church with those very needs.

Sharon: The tune didn't sound difficult, but should we have the congregation sing a new tune and try to pray the words at the same time?

Mark: The choir could sing the stanzas, and we have license to print the refrain for the congregation to join in.

Steve, lay member: In the tradition I come from, the musicians would keep playing softly, and the spoken prayers would begin over the music.

Mark: Well, we could certainly do that. And then let's sing the refrain again following the prayers. Will that work, Sharon?

Sharon: That's just right! May I have a copy of the text? I'd like to weave it into the end of the sermon. We need to be sure that the liturgist of the day is informed about the pattern for the prayers. Mark, can you take care of that?

Several things are noteworthy about this conversation. First, the music director has studied the assigned lectionary texts and knows the resources, and has come to the meeting with musical ideas that will enhance the texts and themes of the day. His suggestion is welcomed by the group, and in turn, Mark is open to ideas for integrating the song into the service. The lay members feel comfortable offering observations and suggestions, including a remembered tradition (hearing music played under the spoken prayers) that is unfamiliar to the current congregation. The pastor has the congregation in mind: "Can they sing this?" She is supportive of and confident in the music director's abilities and quickly sees ways to weave together the words of the sermon and the peoples' response.

Learning the Congregation's Song

Whether you are new to the church you serve or have been the pastoral musician for several years, you will, through your participation in the planning conversations and the reflection sessions, learn much about the congregation's "heart songs," or as Tom Long says, the "reservoir of prayers, creeds, songs, and responses committed to memory."[2] What are the favorites? What styles and genres reflect the language of the people in praise and prayer? As you look again at the list of "important songs" you compile from the worship survey, you may be surprised by what you thought you knew. There may be much more variety in the people's musical language than you assumed. You may note a real curiosity and a desire to learn more about the songs of faith. You may perceive that the congregation is eager to sing songs of the global church or to chant the psalms.

Woven through the story of the songs and those who sing them is the larger story of the congregation. In the planning sessions, you have a chance to hear some of those stories. "Does anyone remember why we always sing this hymn on stewardship Sunday?" "A few years ago the confirmation class sang a beautiful song at the confirmation service. Might we ask this year's class to sing?" Integrating the sung story of this congregation with the songs of the whole church requires that you know the stories and the songs.

So listen, make notes, and incorporate the "heart songs" as well as new repertoire into the rhythms of the seasons.

One way to honor the "heart language" and to live more faithfully into the liturgical year is to tie together the Sundays of a season by singing one or two responses in every service. This small musical ritual, using a phrase appropriate to the season, encourages the congregation's awareness of the liturgical season and draws worshipers into deeper recognition of their own spiritual journey. For example, a congregation might use "I Have Decided to Follow Jesus"—a chorus from the Indian subcontinent that has the flavor of an African American spiritual—during Lent. On the first Sunday in Lent, one stanza could be sung by an unaccompanied vocalist at the beginning of the service. On subsequent Sundays, the congregation might join in, or a solo instrument might play as the people listen, hearing the words as an echo in the soul. Catechumens preparing for baptism (or confirmation) at Easter might sing the song one Sunday as the congregation surrounds them with prayerful support in their time of preparation. Depending on your tradition, the congregation might sing the song before and after the reading of the Gospel, a reminder as worshipers hear the Word that they have been baptized into the journey with Christ. This one familiar heart song can accompany them on their individual and collective way to Jerusalem and Holy Week. You and the members of the planning team will have ideas of songs appropriate for other seasons.

Teaching and Leading the People's Song

In addition to your teaching in the planning and ordering sessions, you may be invited to speak to Sunday school classes and church women's groups, or to lead a Lenten Bible study. Imagine how you might use hymns as the primary texts for these sessions. For example, you can explore the heritage of our faith through the centuries, or analyze the metaphors and images in new texts. Your own curiosity and inquiry into the church's song will be contagious, and the people will join in singing with informed enthusiasm.

Your teaching in these several venues will help prepare the whole congregation to participate as you invite the people to learn and sing new songs—texts written by women or by young writers, ancient texts newly translated, newly composed tunes, and melodies that tie us to Christians of other eras. You will introduce music as prayer response, as acclamation preceding the Gospel reading, as benediction. You will learn songs in unfamiliar languages with new rhythms. Chapter 5 offers guidelines for selecting congregational hymns and songs. The bibliography contains many sources for congregational music.

It was the second week of Lent, but already the team was meeting to begin mapping out the Sundays of Easter. A large chart with all the lectionary readings from Ash Wednesday through Pentecost of Year A hung on the wall of the meeting room. As the meeting began, one member noticed that Psalm 23 was assigned for the Fourth Sunday in Lent and also for the Fourth Sunday of Easter. This discovery initiated a lively conversation with some deeply engaging questions. What does it mean for us to sing those familiar words more than halfway through our journey to the cross? How does it feel to sing that psalm on the other side of Easter, having been through the "valley of the shadow of death"? Katherine, the music minister, led the team in exploring various musical settings of Psalm 23, some familiar, some new, for the congregation. For the Fourth Sunday in Lent, the group chose a beloved and comforting setting—a nineteenth-century paraphrase of the psalm by Henry Baker sung to the tune "St. Columbia." With their newfound insight into the lectionary and the liturgical calendar, the team members agreed that in the season of Resurrection and New Life, the congregation would be ready to learn a new and lively setting of the psalm. Katherine found a setting online: a Haitian folk song with text in both Creole and English. She suggested that the members of the praise group could sing the stanzas and the congregation could join the refrain, singing in Creole or English.

—Planning team of a midsize congregation

All the Musicians in Leadership

Each time you rehearse with the choir, praise team, liturgical cantors, or any ensemble, you are preparing these musicians for their role as leaders of the liturgy. You are empowering them for ministry. Teach *about* the music they are learning—when it was written, the way the composer has set particular words or phrases to enhance the text. Spend one rehearsal each season reading through possible hymns or anthems or service music. Ask open-ended questions about the music, and listen to the responses. "How might we use this song in worship?" "This is a familiar hymn text, but how has the composer helped you understand the images in a new way with this tune?" The more these musicians know about the music, the better they will communicate and lead in worship.

Periodically, spend some rehearsal time in discussion about the worship services and the congregation's musical participation, using the questions outlined in chapter 8. This discussion will affirm the musicians' critical role in the worship life of the congregation and help retain interest in and commitment to their ministry.

Children can become effective music leaders. Whether or not you have an organized children's choir, gather the Sunday school children and teach them a short song in a new language, such as *"Jesu, Tawa Pano"* ("Jesus, We Are Here"), a Shona song from Zimbabwe. Let them lead the song in worship, teaching the congregation. Soon, everyone will be singing a new "favorite." Many Christian-education curriculums contain songs (and recordings) of global music. Helping children serve as leaders gives them an important role in worship, not as "performers" or as "cute," but as full participants in the praise of God.

Early in the fall, we wrote, "We want to know your favorite hymns and worship songs" on large sheets of paper and hung the paper in the most trafficked areas of the seminary. Soon there were long lists of songs ranging from "What a Friend We Have in Jesus" to "Lift High the Cross," "You Are My All in All," "Lead Me, Guide Me," and "How Great Thou Art." During this same time, choirs were starting to rehearse, and instrumentalists (from classically trained violinists to folk guitarists to rock drummers) had signed up to play. Planning teams had formed and were ready to begin their work. This combination—people ready to plan, eager to worship, and prepared to offer their musical gifts—was our incentive for a worship service, "Hymns, Psalms and Spiritual Songs: A Musical Service." The music director led the planning team. The planners selected music from the "favorites" lists, decided on a structure for the service, chose prayers and contacted liturgists to lead them, and assigned musicians and musical groups for the various hymns and songs. There was a brief rehearsal and walkthrough before the service. The worship moved without commentary from one song to the next with prayers interspersed. The effect of the whole was a powerful song of the assembly, a wide circle of praise. All could sing their own songs and were invited to learn and sing the songs of others.

—Office of Worship, Candler School of Theology

Pastoral Musician as Student

The planning conversation will open up many opportunities for music within the worship service, including some you may not have thought of, or that the current order of worship does not include, such as psalm chant or antiphons, a Gospel acclamation, a sung call to prayer, musical responses to petitions, sung responses to the Eucharistic prayer, or a final blessing. Tom Long writes in *Beyond the Worship Wars* of the contrast between worship services with just a few musical "punctuations" and the worship of vital congregations. In the latter, he explains:

> One has the sense of being carried along in the service by music, of music as the thread that ties the flow of the service together. There is simply a lot of music in the worship [service] . . . , and it is used in a variety of ways . . . to gather the people, to reinforce the reading of Scripture and the preaching, to generate a sense of mystery throughout, to cultivate congregational participation, to express thanksgiving and joy, to surround the offerings of the people, and to send the congregation into the world to service.[3]

To introduce and lead additional music in the liturgy, you will need to be familiar with the resources available; you must continue to be a student. As you expand your repertoire of hymns and songs, you will become aware of your own lack of proficiency in some areas. You may need to learn to play or lead or sing in new styles—to move outside a comfortable space. If you are trained in a classical style, learn to play gospel. If you work primarily within contemporary genres, learn some songs from the global church. As you continue to learn and become better prepared, you will gain confidence in teaching others.

You can certainly learn much on your own—practicing your instrument or your conducting skills, exploring online sources, or perusing music from various publishers. But because this is a conversational model of planning, consider options for continued learning that encourage dialogue and interpersonal encounters.

1. *Talk with neighboring music leaders, including those in parishes unlike the one you serve.* The three musicians mentioned at the beginning of the chapter all live in the same community and so might find ways to assist one another in their ministries. Take a look at resources in your own area. If you are in a small parish with a minimal budget, call a music minister in a larger church and ask if you can come look through that parish's music library, or see if you might borrow some music for a short time. If the small choir at your church is singing an anthem that requires a flute and you don't have a flute player in your church, might a neighboring congregation "lend" you a high-school band member for the day? If you are serving in a large congregation, how might you initiate hospitable conversation with musicians in smaller churches? Might you organize a seasonal meeting of other music ministers to share ideas, anthems, and new hymns and songs?

2. *Take lessons.* "Lessons" might be regular instruction on your major instrument, or the "lessons" could be a couple of sessions to sharpen your skills in a particular area. Ask a colleague to give you some pointers on conducting gospel songs, or get assistance in Korean pronunciation from the music director of a Korean church.

3. *Attend workshops and conferences.* Every major denomination has at least one extended workshop or "music week" each year. The music and worship services at these events encompass a

wide range of styles and are led by outstanding practitioners. You will be stimulated and inspired and will return to your own church full of ideas. Ask your church leaders to put the registration cost for the event in the church budget, so that the whole congregation supports your desire and need to continue learning.

The additional benefit of learning in the company of others lies in the community itself. You will discover similar concerns and longings, and will share thoughts and experiences. Your own ministry as a musician will be strengthened as you get to know companions called to the same vocation.

Musician as Pastor

The preceding pages outline an ambitious role for the pastoral musician. If you are a full-time minister of music, you may already be overloaded with multiple choirs and other music groups and with preparation for each Sunday. If you are a part-time or volunteer music leader, all these ideas may seem completely unrealistic. Rather than seeing this process as a demand to attend more meetings or to work longer hours, however, imagine how the conversational model of planning can assist or reshape the work you are already doing.

Begin by caring for yourself, for your own spiritual health. Give attention to your need to practice and study so that you can maintain passion and competence for this ministry. Take seriously the suggestions on the previous pages for learning, for engaging with other musicians, for seeing yourself as a part of a fruitful, creative team.

Imagining something new will require you to eliminate some of the "old." This is an opportunity to rid yourself of unproductive habits like last-minute planning or "doing it all." If you gave up some of the "busywork," how might you direct your energy toward expanding the congregation's song? What are some of your own dreams and hopes for the musical life of the congregation? Write them down, and discuss them with the pastor, other musicians in the church, and worship committee members. As the worship life of the congregation is enriched, you will need more help, and more people will be ready to volunteer. Be prepared to welcome new energy and ideas, and more questions about the liturgy, about the assembly's work of praise.

The thoughts in this chapter are images and suggestions, not answers. They are intended to help orient your thinking toward the new things that God can do in and through your ministry. As you become involved with planning and its lively conversation, as you—and the pastor and the church members themselves—see how music and preaching coordinate to deepen the worship life of the whole assembly, your own identity as "pastoral musician" will become clearer to you and to the congregation.

In this pastoral role, you will lead the assembly in song through all the life stages. I know of several congregations that sing Kathleen Thomerson's Advent hymn "I Want to Walk as a Child of the Light" at the service of baptism ("I want to walk as a child of the light; I want to follow Jesus") and also as a part of the service of death and resurrection ("When we have run with patience the race, we shall know the joy of Jesus.")[4] The hymn testifies to the whole of our baptized life in Christ. Surrounding the departing saint with words sung throughout the seasons of life reminds all those gathered of our part in the Christian story. The gesture connects the hymn text and its context. As we sing the church's story and remember our own stories, we join one great song of praise in life, in death, and in life beyond death.

You are the leader of this song. This is the vocation, the true ministry, of the church musician.

Chapter 10

The Pastor

Initiating the Conversation

Susan and Richard were engaged in conversation at the local ministers' meeting. They both served midsize congregations, "good appointments" in the parlance of their denomination. Both churches were thriving; they were involved in community outreach, had ministries involving multiple generations, and were known for vibrant worship. In their conversation, Richard mentioned his desire to put a worship planning team in place. He had been carrying most of the weight of planning along with the music director, and they were running out of substantive ideas. "I've been doing it all," he said. "I need to expand my own vision for worship at Covenant Church." Susan told him about putting the POWR model in place at her church. She was realistic: establishing the model had required a good deal of time at the outset—organizing, recruiting, and training members of the planning teams. But through the process, she had gained confidence in her own authority and had learned to trust the work of the people. She said, "I am energized by the process. Each planning session brings new insights into the preaching texts, new ideas for expressing the themes of the day, and new knowledge of the people I am called to lead."

If you are the pastor, you may see some of your desires and concerns expressed in this dialogue. Whatever your denomination or faith community, you are called, set aside, and ordained in ministry to teach and preach the Word, bring others to Christ, administer the sacraments, and order the life of the congregation. Within that sacred trust, this conversational model is a call to a more collaborative style of worship planning and leadership, a new way of ordering the worship life of the assembly.

This model of planning, as presented, does not eliminate the pastor's voice, wisdom, or responsibility. The pastor's leadership is essential. The model does challenge both pastor and people to communicate more clearly, to question more profoundly, and to listen more intently as the Spirit of God speaks to and through the people. This method assists the pastor in the tasks of Word, sacrament, and order for which the pastor is ordained. Liturgical theologian and pastor Gordon Lathrop has written that the pastor's primary responsibility is to:

> Help the assembly stay strongly centered on the central matters, on the book and the meal and the sending to the hungry, not on our own menu of tastes in music or style, not on the charismatic leader or the charismatic band or the charismatic organ, not on whatever cliches we may have for "going to church." Help the assembly open its doors. Help it welcome everyone, old hand and the newest inquirer alike, to the dignity of being a participant in the assembly of God.[1]

This statement is a call for shared leadership and responsibility; the pastor is charged with helping the people do their work. The conversational planning model outlined in this book can be facilitated by laypeople. But you, as the pastor, will need to introduce the process and demonstrate your own commitment to the practice.

The Pastor and the POWR model

If you have been used to "doing it all," and if the people have started expecting you to do so, it is essential that you bring the laypeople, musicians, and other leaders into the conversation as partners. Introducing a new worship planning practice carries some risk. One pastor wrote, "At first the members did not seem very interested in participating. They said, 'worship is fine the way it is' or, 'planning is your job, Pastor.'" If you encounter some resistance, follow the lead of another pastor, who says, "If someone asked my advice, I would start by telling that person to know the congregation. In most churches, I suspect the model would have to be introduced slowly, say a few services or a season at a time. Find four to seven people and structure a planning conversation in which they can participate." The success of an initial conversation, a taste of this "new thing," can go a long way in building the confidence of pastor and the people. Then determine which of the structures outlined in chapter 3 will work best for your congregation.

Working Together

As we have said throughout this book, the conversational model of worship planning is based on the belief that the Spirit works in and through our speaking and attentive listening. Our conversation in planning and preparing to worship can be a deep and revealing encounter with the Holy. The pastoral musician is a partner in this holy work. Often musicians and pastors are not at odds, but are simply on parallel tracks. By the very nature of their ministries, they use different media and language to draw meaning from word and speech, text and music. But both are passionate about their callings and are committed to excellence in the worship of God. The questions in the POWR process can help you find a common language of leadership and a common purpose in leading the liturgy.

Working together, you and the pastoral musician and the members of the planning team will discover a common joy in exploring the Scripture texts. You will be surprised by new ideas generated in conversation with those who think differently than you do. You will gain insights into the spirit (and the spiritual life) of the congregation. You will feed your own hungers as you engage in meaningful conversation about the central things of our life and faith. You will hear people's life stories told in relation to the biblical stories. You will listen to stories from the "edges" of the congregation—stories from the world outside the church walls where people are in ministry in their daily work.

> Worship planning used to mean filling in the slots of the bulletin that change every week. Through this new model of planning and ordering and reflecting, it became a means of grace. God was

given the opportunity to speak to us through the Scriptures and the conversation around the table. In some ways, worship planning itself has become a worship service.

—JOHN, PASTOR OF A SMALL RURAL CHURCH

Inviting and Leading

The pastor's work of preaching and teaching and ordering the liturgical life of the congregation is a ministry of inclusion. You are making a way for the people, preparing them for gathering and hearing, feasting at the table, and serving in the world. As Lathrop writes:

> These three things may help us to think about the spirituality of the pastor: the pastor learns the important tasks by heart . . . then the pastor imagines the meaning of the assembly using all the central things (the font, the book, the Holy Meal) to do so. Then, at every turn, the pastor tries to give access to others.[2]

This access is a primary characteristic of the conversational model. The structure and the planning and ordering invite participation by many of the people and ultimately by all the gathered assembly in worship. The previous chapters outline the steps and structures. The pastor will be the key person in organizing the process for the congregation and will lead the meetings until the lay members are trained and confident. You will continue to have a major leadership role as the pastor. Your work of inviting, listening, teaching, and guiding the process is critical.

The POWR model brought something different. With "P" the first week, we had space to breathe in the text and live in it. And "O" the next week allowed time to process and to think. The idea of reflecting intentionally on our worship was an amazing thing; the remembrance itself was a holy moment. At first in my church, the folks were a bit intimidated, but then they picked up on what I was doing: "Hey, that's kind of fun." I didn't set harsh boundaries, but set softer metaphorical boundaries that created more freedom for people. It's a very playful process, and I think that's why we have such a good time.

—RANDALL, PASTOR OF A RURAL CONGREGATION

Benefits for the Pastor

Introducing a new worship planning process requires significant time and energy. But doing so can have multiple benefits for the pastor and the pastor's ministry.

1. *Your preaching will be enriched.* If you are already in a lectionary study group, you know the value of discussing the lectionary texts with colleagues. Likewise, the planning team conversations will uncover questions about the central things of your own life and faith as well as the people's. You will see new details in the Scripture readings; you will learn new hymns; you will gain new insights into the minds and hearts of your parishioners. The sermons you preach will draw on and perhaps elaborate all these discoveries.

2. *You will be more accountable for the work of preaching and leading worship.* Scott, the senior pastor of a large church, says, "This practice makes me better prepared. It keeps me disciplined. I cannot wait until Saturday to put a sermon together, hoping the music director has either chosen some songs that will connect with the message or can be flexible on the spot. I know that when our planning team meets, members depend on me to be prepared and to lead them in the study of the scriptural texts."

3. *You will have more time to prepare.* That sounds contradictory, since we just mentioned the amount of time required to initiate and organize the process. But once the teams are in place, you will learn to trust those who complete the planning and ordering, the training and rehearsing. You can let go of the details and focus on preparation for the work to which you are called.

4. *You will be supported in your work of preparing for worship.* Because you have shared the preaching texts with the planners, have used the texts in Bible study, or have published the lectionary listings on the church's website, members of the congregation can

be reading and praying those same texts during the week. As you are prayerfully writing the sermon or outlining the prayers of intercession, you will realize that you are upheld by members of the congregation who are themselves students of the Word.

> Prior to launching the planning team, I did not use the lectionary regularly. Within the first few weeks, I became an avid lectionary proponent. I began to see the lectionary as the map for me to use in guiding my congregation through the church year. By making this journey year after year, traveling with a different Gospel as the guide every three years, we come to better understand who we are as Christians. Using the lectionary, our congregants saw a new interpretation of the story, one that can help them grow in Christian knowledge and experience.
>
> —MIKE, PASTOR OF A SMALL-TOWN CHURCH

---

5. *You will be more effective in teaching.* Many pastors use Bible study classes or other teaching opportunities to discuss the upcoming preaching texts. The planning conversations will generate interest in additional study about worship: the themes of the Christian year, the sacraments, or your liturgical heritage; and, in turn, your teaching on these subjects will relate directly to the worship planning. Jan, the pastor of a small congregation, says, "It's the one thing we don't talk about enough: *Why* do we . . . stand for the Gospel, exchange the peace? I want them to do more than participate in the tradition. I want them to *know* the tradition."

6. *You will be a better worshiper.* Others are in leadership with you; you can trust their preparation as you trust your own. You are gathered *with* the people in the presence of God.

Pastor, Priest, Prophet

Empowered by the planning process and supported by the work of the congregation, you will see your roles in liturgical leadership more clearly. You are pastor and priest—and also prophet. This planning model allows the prophetic role to operate in strong tension with the other two. Ordained pastors, by virtue of that common title, know themselves to be the guides, the shepherds, the ones who care for the people. The pastor leads from within the circumstances of the congregation, looking inward and outward for dangers, for moments to teach, to care for, and to gather those people entrusted to her. Most pastors also know their strong role as priest—the one who is with and before the people gathered in the presence of God, the one who leads the people in speaking to God, who speaks for the people to God, and who presides with authority.

The model of conversational, covenantal preparation for worship also elicits the role of the ordained minister as prophet. The prophet moves to the edge of the conversation, into the concerns, difficulties, and debates, and interprets and communicates to the congregation a vision of God's "new thing." The prophet helps the people articulate their longings and dreams and leads the congregation in making them reality. Because this model engages the people in the imaginative readings of the texts and in the creative work of identifying and inviting the talents of the congregation, the clergy are freed to step back and view the "big picture," to celebrate what is yet to come, to be the prophetic voice of the congregation.

Through the planning process, all are working toward what Lathrop calls "a freedom to begin to see that liturgy is not in the book but in the present actions of the assembly."[3] Ultimately, the work of planning and ordering, gathering for worship and reflecting, gives the people of the assembly grace to see more clearly who they are and who they are becoming as the body of Christ. Leading this work is the pastor's task.

Pay attention to the small things, and give thanks. The Holy One is in your midst. Jon, a young pastor, recounted, "As they dipped the bread into the wine, the difficulties of my life were slowly pulled into perspective. I remember thinking, 'This is what it's about—serving people, loving them, sharing life, and being glad for one another.' It was a truly moving moment for me."

God is doing a new thing! Do you not perceive it?

Epilogue

The planning team had gathered for a final reflection session. Its year of service was completed, and the members were rotating off the team. They agreed that their work had been transformative for the congregation and for their own spiritual lives as well. When pressed to elaborate, Cezanne said:

> When I first joined the team, I didn't feel equipped at all, because I had never planned worship before, but being around all the other enthusiastic team members gave me confidence. I was ready to give it a go! We all had the same objective—we wanted the service to be a beautiful offering for God. We wanted people to feel it was worth it to come. And now I am aware of everything in worship—the relationship of the music and preaching, the movement within the service, the congregation's responses, the arrangement of the chairs, the position of the table. I'm aware of everything! Because as a worshiper, I now see that these details affect the way people worship. I will never be the same!

As you conclude a season or a year of team planning with the conversational planning model, take time to reflect on the process and the worship life of the congregation. Consider the ways this model has increased the spiritual maturity of the people who have planned and ordered and reflected, and all those who have worshiped. Discover how people's lives have been enriched, blessed by this process. Many will never be the same.

From small congregations and large, we have heard the stories of renewed sacramental life, growing interest in studying the

Christian year, expanded repertoire of hymns and songs, increased participation in prayer—practices that deepened worshipers' faith, that answered unspoken questions about life in the presence and the love of God. One woman on a planning team spoke of her experience this way. "On a personal level, I developed close friendships with the other committee members and the pastor. I discovered my identity within the congregation and became a more active member. Ultimately, I found that my faith had deepened, and I had a more dynamic relationship with God."

Through participation in the process and in enriched worship, people do find a place and an identity within the congregation and the whole salvation story. Nate, a pastor, said:

> Our church is full of stories of people finding a place where they can give expression to their stories and to a faith that is beginning to shape those stories. The POWR model allows people to engage the Scriptures at a depth they would not otherwise achieve and offers them ownership of our practice of worship. My experience is that this is pretty rare for most individuals.

In every place, the POWR model has expanded the conversation among members of the congregation, their pastors, and musicians. Another planning team member noted:

> More and more voices are incorporated into worship, more people are invested in the expected excellence of worship, and there is a new sense of excitement about what's going to happen this week and how that experience will help them create a stronger connection to God and to one another.

And within this ongoing conversation, there are moments of revelation. Jonathan shares:

> Last night was a real turning point in the process, because our praise group began talking about the intended outcome of our worship, how it could move people and immerse them in the text. This is what we have been trying to do all along—to provide individuals with opportunities to access Scripture, live in it, dwell on it, and come away with a new and deeper understanding

> of God's love and redemption. I was floored by the conversation, the fun we've been having, and the amazing ways that God is working in this place.

Worshiping with the assembly and reflecting in the company of the faithful can be life-changing. We may never be the same.

These brief reports testify to transforming experiences. But you need not take our word for it. Attend to the conversation in your own church. While some results of the process are quantifiable—for example, that the attendance has increased, or a new choir has formed—other effects are more subtle. Listen to individual stories, to the ways people speak about worship. How are people reflecting on, talking about, and living out their encounters with the risen Christ in the worshiping assembly? In what ways are they more engaged with Scripture? How are they attentive and responsive to the language of prayer and the metaphors of hymns? Are they learning to appreciate and accept one another? Do they see Christ in the stranger? All these are questions of formation, or attitude. The responses to these questions reveal measurable growth into the likeness of Christ.

The precise outcome of this growth will be unique to your congregation. Some congregations will notice dramatic changes; others will celebrate small steps. Don Saliers, liturgical theologian and mentor of many pastors, has often used the phrase "humanity at full stretch before God" in referring to the assembly fully engaged in prayer and praise. To be "at full stretch" is the welcome challenge of the questions in this book and of the model of planning, ordering, worshiping, and reflecting. If you enter into the process, you and your congregation will be stretched—stretched to see the Spirit of God already working among you. And in response, you and others will be drawn to imagine worship as one great song of praise and thanksgiving, of awe and wonder, of confession and restoration. The people of God will know themselves in the renewing and sustaining feast that sends them into a world in need. In truth, you will be pulled into new and surprising and life-giving encounters with the Holy One, as together you plan and order the service, gather for worship, and reflect on the liturgy, the work of all the people.

Amen. May it be so.

Appendix A

Worship Survey

Name: (optional)

Please describe your experience of worshiping at *(name of church or community)* by completing these sentences in any way that seems appropriate to you.

Worship

1. A word or phrase that best describes my experience of worship at our church is
2. I participate in worship at our church by
3. The most engaging act of worship for me is
4. When we celebrate Holy Communion, I
5. In hearing the Word read and preached, I
6. The music during worship at our church is
7. Some hymns or songs that are particularly important to me or to this congregation include

The Community

1. The people who come to worship here
2. People are welcomed by
3. The most important part of worship for this congregation is
4. We learn about opportunities to assist in worship leadership through

Questions and Comments

1. I have always wondered why we
2. If I could make any change in the worship service, I would
3. Worship would be more engaging or inviting if
4. Additional comments or questions:

Appendix B

Leader's Guide for Planning

Date of worship service:
Liturgical season:
Lectionary (or preaching) texts:
Preacher/presider:
Sermon theme:

Before the Planning Session

1. Send texts to the planning team members.
2. Gather resources.

Phase I: Thinking about the Text

1. What words and phrases do you hear when you read the texts aloud? What images and themes are evoked? What surprises you?
2. What emotions are generated by these readings? How do you feel (comforted, joyous, concerned, angry)?
3. How do the themes and images look, sound, and feel (bright, dark, loud, lonely, smooth, jagged, etc.)?
4. What other senses are engaged by this text?
5. How might we understand these images and themes in the context of the liturgical season?

Phase II: Concrete Ideas

1. What sounds do you hear in worship this day (Is the music lively? Contemplative? Festive? What words and phrases from hymns and songs come to mind?
2. What gestures and movements are summoned by our reading of the texts? A solemn procession? A dance? Movement to the altar rail for prayer?
3. What visual expressions are suggested by the texts? Banners? An arrangement at the entrance? Or on the windowsills? How will we arrange the space in which we worship?

At the Conclusion of the Planning Session

1. Assign tasks (contacting volunteer leaders, making special altar arrangements, designing visuals, preparing drama, etc.).
2. Distribute planning notes to team members, pastor, and music minister.
3. Continue to communicate by e-mail regarding tasks completed, new ideas, or refinement of brainstorming thoughts.

Organizing the Notes

To sort the many ideas and suggestions, the scribe may arrange them by categories, or may begin to place them within a broad outline of the worship service. You might use both options or a combination, depending on the direction of the conversation or the way ideas focus on a particular part of the service.

Option I: Categories

Option 1 clusters the suggestions according to the broad elements of the service: word, music, movement, and visual expression. It will help gather many ideas but resists putting them immediately into a linear order. This plan works well if you want to generate ideas for an entire season or if you want to encourage multiple suggestions in each category.

TEXTS
Presenting Scripture
Leading prayers

MUSIC
Hymns and songs
Music by the choir or praise team
Instrumental music
Service music: psalms, prayers, responses, communion setting

MOVEMENT AND GESTURE
Processions
Dance
Other (particular seasonal rituals; e.g., lighting the Advent wreath)

VISUALS/MEDIA
Seasonal paraments
Flower arrangements
Other designs or arrangements (entrance table, windows, etc.)
Banners
Video/projected art
Other

Option 2: The *ordo*

Option 2 places the multiple suggestions within the general order of the service. This option for organizing the planning notes works well if the group is engaged in learning about the *ordo* and the flow of the worship service, or if the ideas are centered on a particular part of the service; for example, a seasonal procession or a renewal of baptism in response to the Word.

GATHERING TO PRAISE GOD
Hymns/songs/instrumental music
Prayers
Movement/procession
Visual/media

HEARING GOD'S WORD
Scripture texts (way of presenting)
Music
Sermon (theme, title)

RESPONDING IN FAITH/COMING TO THE TABLE
Prayers
Offering
Holy Communion
Other responses

DEPARTING TO BE THE CHURCH IN THE WORLD
Prayers
Music
Movement/procession

Appendix C

Leader's Guide for Ordering

Before the Meeting

1. Scribe sends the notes from the planning session.
2. Keep assignments and ideas going on e-mail.
3. Ask the team members to reread the Scripture texts and planning notes to be prepared to make decisions.
4. Scribe prepares a rough outline of the bulletin from which the planners will work.

Review and Report

1. Review the texts, sermon theme, and suggestions from the planning meeting.
2. Report on assignments (specific tasks, personnel, logistics).

Order the Worship Service

1. What do we need to do to make space for God's spirit? Which of the ideas suggested best reflect the message of God's Word this day?
2. Finalize music, prayers, and the reading of Scripture.
3. Attend to other logistical issues and details.

Seeing the Whole

1. Talk through the whole service using the bulletin as a guide, paying attention to the smooth flow of the liturgy.
2. Fill in any blanks, or direct any questions to the appropriate person.
3. Make final assignments for the team members.

Move into the Worship Space

1. Check any final logistical or technical details.
2. Pray for those who will gather for worship.

By the End of This Session

1. Bulletin (or script) is completed and sent to pastor for final editing.
2. Final assignments of details or needed communication.

Order for a Service of Word and Table (Holy Communion)

This *ordo,* with slight variations, is in broad use across many denominations. This outline will show you the many options for ordering the worship service in your congregation.

Gathering

The people assemble in the name of the Risen Christ, to give praise to God through the power of the Holy Spirit.

Music as the people gather

Words of welcome and greeting

Hymn or songs

Opening prayer

Confession and pardon and signs of reconciliation (The inclusion and placement depends on the denominational practice and the season of the year.)

Hearing God's Word

The people participate in hearing God's Word read, sung, and spoken.

A prayer for illumination
The lessons
Old Testament (or First) Lesson
Psalm
Epistle (or Second) Lesson
Hymn or song or anthem or Gospel acclamation
Gospel Lesson
The sermon

Responding in Faith:

Having heard God's Word, we are invited to pray for the world, to offer our gifts, and to join the Feast.

The Creed (depending on the denomination)
Prayers of the people or pastoral prayer
Confession and pardon and signs of reconciliation (if not part of the gathering)
Offering our gifts
The Holy Communion
The prayer of consecration
The Lord's Prayer
The fraction (the breaking of the bread)
The distribution of the elements
Prayer after communing

Departing

Having sung, prayed, listened, and feasted together, the people are sent to be the body of Christ for the world.

Hymn or song
Blessing and dismissal
Music as we depart

Appendix D

Sample Customaries for Worship Leaders

Guidelines (or customaries) for lay ministers in the liturgy offer simple instructions for those who serve. You will want to develop guidelines in conversation with the coordinator or chair of the ministry areas and the pastor. The guidelines for each ministry should state:

1. Why this ministry is important.
2. Where to find the needed materials (robes, Bible, candle lighters, offering plates, etc.).
3. The sequence of the person's work in the service.
4. Where to store materials or vestments after the service.
5. Any other details particular to your setting.

Sacristans and Altar Guild Members

Altar guild members or sacristans prepare the communion elements, the altar, and the pulpit area, as well as the worship space in general. This ministry is essential for the congregation's reverence of Word and Sacrament.

Where to Find Things

1. Communion vessels are in lower-left cabinets.
2. Fair linens (white altar cloths) are in the top drawer of the linen chest.

3. Purificators (square white napkins for covering the elements or for holding the bread as it is served) are in boxes on the shelf in the sacristy.
4. Candle lighter is in the cabinet in the corner. The lighter and extra wicks are on the shelf in the same cabinet.
5. Bread bakers will bring the bread to the sacristy and place it on the counter. Juice and wine are in the sacristy cabinet. (Make note on the chart on the door when items are running low.)

Before the Service

1. See that the Bible is open to the correct passage.
2. Put a small glass of water in the pulpit shelf for the preacher.
3. Replace any candles that are shorter than three inches. (New candles are in the lower-left cabinet in the sacristy.) See that the wicks are ready for lighting.
4. Place the fair linens on the altar, the table beside the altar, and the credence table at the entrance.
5. Place the bookstand on the left side of the altar. With the presider, determine which eucharistic prayers will be used for the day. Turn to the correct page in the sacramentary (or missal).
6. Place unbroken loaves of bread on the paten. Cover the bread with a purificator. Place the paten with bread on the credence table at the entrance.
7. Put wine in the flagon (the pitcher). Put any additional chalices (to be filled after the consecration) on the table beside the altar. Place the flagon beside the paten on the credence table at the entrance.
8. Put the purificators on the small table beside the altar.

After the Service

1. Consume all remaining elements or return them to the earth.
2. Wash and dry all vessels and place them in the storage cabinet.

3. Remove linens from sanctuary. Put clean ones in drawers and soiled ones in the box marked "laundry" in the sacristy.

Readers and Liturgists

Readers and liturgists are lay ministers of the Word. They read the Scripture texts and lead the people in prayer. Their clear and articulate reading conveys the importance of the living Word of God.

Before the Service

1. Practice reading the Scripture or prayers aloud before the day of the service. Listen to the sound of the phrases, noting words that should be emphasized. Check the pronunciation of difficult words or names.
2. Read aloud in the worship space, so that you are familiar with the microphones and the resonance of the sound. Speak the living Word of God clearly, with attention to its importance. Do not rush; speak more slowly than your normal conversational pace.

During Worship

1. You will be seated with the congregation on the lectern side.
2. Be sure you have a copy of any written prayers.
3. The large pulpit Bible is large-print NRSV. It will be marked with the text assigned.
4. If you are leading a responsive psalm or reading, give clear instructions (e.g., "The men will read the light print; the women will read the bold print" or "We will sing response A"). Use declarative or imperative verb forms and minimal words.
5. When reading Scripture, announce the text saying, "A reading from the . . . chapter of . . . , beginning with the . . . verse" or "The Gospel of our Lord, according to Saint . . . ," or as you are instructed. At the end of the reading, say

"This is the Word of God for the people of God," or "The Word of God," or as you are instructed.

Communion Servers

Communion servers assist at the communion feast. Their quiet gestures of respect for the sacrament and those communing will ensure that all are welcomed at the table.

Before the Service

1. Wash your hands.
2. Vest in white alb and cincture.
3. Servers sit together in the front row facing the altar.

During the Service

1. At the offertory or presentation, move in a single line to your assigned place near or behind the altar.
2. After the elements are consecrated, you will be served the bread and wine. Then the deacon will hand the bread and chalice to those serving, or may direct you to take the elements from the altar.
3. Proceed to your stations as assigned by the deacon.
4. Break a small piece of bread from the loaf and place it in the hands of the communicant, saying: "The body of Christ, broken for you," or "This is the body of Christ," or as you have been directed.
5. Hold the chalice so that the communicant can touch the bread to the wine or sip the wine, saying: "This is the blood of Christ shed for you," or "The blood of Christ, the cup of salvation," or as you have been directed.
6. After all have been served, return to the altar and wait for the deacon to direct you to the sacristy. Put all elements on the counter and cover with the purificators. Return to your seat, either before the final prayer or during the hymn. Do not return during the prayer.

After the Service

1. Hang up your alb. If it is soiled, put it in the hamper for laundering.

Appendix E

Leader's Guide for Reflecting

Before the Reflection Session

Be sure all team members have a bulletin from the service. The scribe may order the notes according to the main points of discussion: God's presence, our work, and recommendations.

Remembering God's Presence with Us

In our worship how did we encounter the faithful work of God, the presence of the risen Christ, and the life-giving power of the Holy Spirit?

1. What words would you use to describe this time of worship?
2. How did you perceive the Spirit of God moving among us? What did you see, hear, taste, smell, and touch?
3. In what ways did you hear the Good News of Christ? What made the Word of God come alive? (music, speech, silence, visuals, etc.)
4. How was the congregation challenged and/or strengthened in this time of worship?
5. Were there elements of surprise? If so, what were they?
6. In what ways were the people attentive and participating?
7. How are the members of our congregation growing closer to God and to one another through worship?
8. How are we being equipped to be the body of Christ in the world?

Reflecting on our Work in Worship

1. How were we hospitable to neighbor and welcoming of the stranger?
2. In what ways did we offer hospitality to all?
3. How did our preparation enable the work of all the people, the liturgy?
4. Did all the elements of the service (hymns and songs, prayer words and postures, visual designs, and other sensory experiences) support the message of the scriptural texts?
5. Did the service flow smoothly and coherently?
6. Were the leaders effectively equipped? Readers? Servers? Ushers? Others? Were there any impediments to their leadership in this service? What improvements should we make?
7. Was the technology helpful? Was the sound clear and articulate? Was the lighting adequate? Was the video engaging, not distracting? Were the print materials easy to read?
8. Did we use the space wisely? Could people (processions, dancers, drama participants, leaders) get where they needed to go? Were the visual elements easily seen and understood?
9. What other details are worth noting?

Recommendations

1. Practices to continue.
2. Issues to be aware of.
3. Larger concerns.

After the Session

1. Scribe sends notes to the pastor and the team.
2. If this is the end of the term of service for the planning team, send notes of appreciation.

Notes

Chapter 1: Worship and the People

1. Delores Dufner, “God, You Call Us to This Place”; copyright © 1987, 1993, The Sisters of St. Benedict; admin. OCP Publications; found in *Sing! A New Creation* (Grand Rapids: Calvin Institute of Christian Worship, 2001) and other recent hymnals.

2. Thomas G. Long, *Beyond the Worship Wars: Building Vital and Faithful Worship* (Bethesda: Alban Institute, 2001), 21.

3. Jane Rogers Vann, *Gathered Before God: Worship-Centered Church Renewal* (Louisville: Westminster John Knox, 2004), 65*ff.*

4. Saliers credits the origins of this concept to liturgical theologian James F. White.

5. From the Great Thanksgiving (ecumenical, Protestant).

6. *The United Methodist Hymnal: Book of United Methodist Worship* (Nashville: United Methodist Publishing House, 1989), 11.

7. From “A Statement of Faith of the United Church of Canada”; see *The United Methodist Hymnal* (1989), 883.

Chapter 3: The Planning Team

1. Corinne Ware, *Discover Your Spiritual Type* (Bethesda: Alban Institute, 1995), preface.

2. Ware, *Discover Your Spiritual Type,* 31.

3. Doris Akers, “Sweet, Sweet Spirit” (1962); copyright © 1962, Manna Music, Inc.

4. *The Book of Common Prayer* (New York: Church Hymnal Corporation, 1979), 366.

Chapter 4: Planning

1. Gordon Lathrop and Timothy J. Wengert, *Christian Assembly: Marks of the Church in a Pluralistic Age* (Minneapolis: Fortress, 2004), 8.

Chapter 7: Worship

1. *The Book of Common Prayer.*

2. Isaac Watts (1674-1748), “My Shepherd Will Supply My Need;” paraphrase of Psalm 23.

Chapter 8: Reflecting

1. Gordon W. Lathrop, *Holy Things: A Liturgical Theology* (Minneapolis: Augsburg Fortress, 1993), 6.

Chapter 9: Musicians

1. Marty Haugen, “Healer of Our Every Ill;” text and music copyright © 1987, GIA Publications, Inc.

2. Long, *Beyond the Worship Wars,* 89.

3. Long, *Beyond the Worship Wars,* 61.

4. Kathleen Thomerson, “I Want to Walk as a Child of the Light” (1966); words and music copyright © 1970, 1975, Celebration.

Chapter 10: The Pastor

1. Lathrop and Wengert, *Christian Assembly,* 16.

2. Gordon Lathrop, *The Pastor: A Spirituality* (Minneapolis: Fortress, 2006), 25.

3. Lathrop, *The Pastor,* 25.

Bibliography

Resources for Planning and Leadership Worship

Understanding Christian Worship

Introductions to the theology and practice of worship and the sacraments

Felton, Gayle Carlton. *This Holy Mystery: A United Methodist Understanding of Holy Communion.* Nashville: Discipleship Resources, 2005. Also online at http://www.gbod.org/worship/thm-bygc.pdf.

Broad theological principles and practical details. Essential reading for United Methodist pastors and congregations.

Foley, Edward. *From Age to Age: How Christians Have Celebrated the Eucharist.* Chicago: Liturgical Training Publications, 1991.

Traces the history of communion practices through architecture, music, texts, and vessels. Stories and illustrations make this history informative and accessible.

Lathrop, Gordon W. *Holy Things: A Liturgical Theology.* Minneapolis: Augsburg Fortress, 1993.

A foundational text in liturgical theology and reflections on the meaning of Christian liturgy.

———. *Central Things: Worship in Word and Sacrament.* Minneapolis: Augsburg Fortress, 2005.

Describes the distinctive practices of Christian worship and their theological importance. One of a series of small, helpful books published by Augsburg Fortress for congregational study.

Ramshaw, Gail. *A Three-Year Banquet: The Lectionary for the Assembly.* Minneapolis: Augsburg Fortress, 2004.

A look at the development of the lectionary, and ways that its use is a formative resource for congregations. One of a series of small, helpful books published by Augsburg Fortress for congregational study.

———. *The Three-Day Feast: Maundy Thursday, Good Friday, Easter.* Minneapolis: Augsburg Fortress, 2004.
Describes how celebrating the Triduum can deepen the theological understanding of the congregation. One of a series of small, helpful books published by Augsburg Fortress for congregational study.

Saliers, Don E. *Worship Come to Its Senses.* Nashville: Abingdon, 1996.
Focuses on the four "senses" of worship: awe, delight, truth, and hope.

Stookey, Laurence Hull. *Calendar: Christ's Time for the Church.* Nashville: Abingdon, 1996.
Traces the history of the Christian year and describes its theological significance. Good teaching material for small groups.

Torvend, Samuel. *Daily Bread, Holy Meal: Opening the Gifts of Holy Communion.* Minneapolis: Augsburg Fortress, 2004.
Encourages communities to understand the connections between their celebration of the Eucharist and their everyday lives. One of a series of small, helpful books published by Augsburg Fortress for congregational study.

Issues in Worship Practice and Planning

Books that address specific concerns and issues in congregational worship

Abbington, W. James. *Let Mt. Zion Rejoice! Music in the African American Church.* Valley Forge: Judson Press, 2001.
A challenge for musical excellence in African American churches, and encouragement for pastors and musicians.

Carson, Timothy L. *Transforming Worship.* St. Louis: Chalice Press, 2003.
Includes historical, contemporary, and theological explanations of Christian worship and suggests ways to improve the worship life of the community.

Hawn, C. Michael. *One Bread, One Body: Exploring Cultural Diversity in Worship.* Herndon, Va.: Alban Institute, 2003.

A guide to multicultural worship. Includes theological reflection, case studies, and practical suggestions.

Lathrop, Gordon W., and Timothy J. Wengert. *Christian Assembly: Marks of the Church in a Pluralistic Age*. Minneapolis: Fortress, 2004.
Discusses the defining practices and "marks" of the church and its historic practices in dialogue with contemporary social and congregational culture.

Long, Thomas G. *Beyond the Worship Wars: Building Vital and Faithful Worship*. Bethesda, Md.: Alban Institute, 2001.
Explores why people worship and describes how a variety of factors (music, space, community, leadership) affect Christian worship.

Plantinga, Cornelius, Jr., and Sue A. Rozeboom. *Discerning the Spirits: A Guide to Thinking about Christian Worship Today*. Grand Rapids: Eerdmanns, 2003.
Overview of theological issues surrounding worship planning. A thoughtful inquiry into the intersection of worship and culture.

Ray, David R. *Wonderful Worship in Smaller Churches*. Cleveland: Pilgrim Press, 2000.
An encouraging and pastorally insightful look at the smaller congregation and its particular characteristics and needs in worship.

Vann, Jane Rogers. *Gathered Before God: Worship-Centered Church Renewal*. Louisville: Westminster John Knox, 2004.
Case studies illumine the exploration of worship as the pattern for congregational life, learning, and formation.

Ware, Corinne. *Discover Your Spiritual Type*. Bethesda: Alban Institute, 1995.
Examines different ways communities and individuals understand worship (their spiritual types) and suggests how worship planners might take into account this diversity. Includes a helpful spiritual type inventory for small groups or congregations.

Forming Worship Leaders

The roles of ordained and designated leaders (pastors, deacons, church musicians, etc.) in the congregation and tools for their formation as worship leaders

Anderson, E. Byron, ed. *Worship Matters: A United Methodist Guide to Worship Work,* vol. II. Nashville: Discipleship Resources, 1999.

Focuses on the details of worship leadership, space, and planning, with helpful sections addressed to various lay worship leaders: ushers, readers, acolytes, and others.

Begolly, Michael J. *Leading the Assembly in Prayer,* rev. ed. San Jose, Calif.: Resource Publications, 2008.

Roman Catholic guide for laity and ordained clergy leading the assembly. Helpful spiritual preparation for leading/presiding.

Day Miller, Barbara. *The New Pastor's Guide to Leading Worship.* Nashville: Abingdon, 2006.

Introduces new pastors to the art of leading worship and the habits of good worship leaders.

Duck, Ruth C. *Finding Words for Worship: A Guide for Leaders.* Louisville: Westminster John Knox, 1995.

Concise, creative guide to writing public prayers and other liturgical texts.

Farlee, Robert Buckley, and Eric Vollen, eds. *Leading the Church's Song.* Minneapolis: Augsburg Fortress, 1998.

A collection of practical essays on leading, interpreting, and accompanying music for worship. Includes helpful CD with examples.

Lathrop, Gordon. *The Pastor: A Spirituality.* Minneapolis: Fortress, 2006.

A theological reflection on the role of the ordained leader in worship, both devotional and practical in its approach.

Long, Kimberly Bracken. *The Worshiping Body: The Art of Leading Worship.* Louisville: Westminster John Knox, 2009.

Grounded in the physicality of worship and the appropriate gestures and attitudes for those who lead and preside in worship.

Sheer, Greg. *The Art of Worship: A Musician's Guide to Leading Modern Worship.* Grand Rapids: Baker Books, 2006.

A detailed guide for introducing, planning, organizing, and rehearsing music and musicians. Helpful chapters on building repertoire and adapting standard hymns in contemporary context.

Springer, Janice Jean. *Nurturing Spiritual Depth in Christian Worship: Ten Practices.* San Jose, Calif.: Resource Publications, 2005.

Offers strategies that can be adopted by diverse communities within a variety of worship styles.

Westermeyer, Paul. *The Church Musician.* Minneapolis: Augsburg Fortress, 1997.
The identity and role of the one leading the church's music. Important book for any church musician, congregations hiring musicians, and pastors working with musicians.

Willimon, William H. *Pastor: The Theology and Practice of Ordained Ministry.* Nashville: Abingdon, 2002.
A United Methodist bishop's reflective and encouraging look at ordained ministry and the roles of the clergy.

Woods, Robert, and Brian Walrath, eds. *The Message in the Music: Studying Contemporary Praise and Worship.* Nashville: Abingdon, 2007.
A thoughtful collection of essays examining the textual and musical aspects of the most popular contemporary worship songs. Helpful criteria for evaluating contemporary praise music.

Planning Worship

A selection of resources for worship planners

General Resources

Sundays and Seasons: A Guide to Worship Planning. Minneapolis: Augsburg Fortress, 2009.
A yearly publication that follows the liturgical calendar and the three-year Revised Common Lectionary. Includes a fine selection of prayers for every Sunday and feast day and practical suggestions about preparing for each liturgical season. Also on-line: www.sundaysandseasons.com.

Bock, Susan K. *Liturgy for the Whole Church: Multigenerational Resources for Worship.* New York: Church Publishing, 2008.
A selection of prayers, songs, dramatic readings, and paraphrases of Scripture texts designed to engage a variety of ages and encourage the participation of children in worship.

Bone, David L., and Mary J. Scifres. *Prepare! A Weekly Worship Planbook for Pastors and Musicians.* Nashville: Abingdon, 2009-2010.

A yearly resource that runs from September to August. Follows the lectionary for each week with all texts printed, and suggestions for hymns and songs, anthems, visuals, and prayers.

Gaddy, Weldon, and Don W. Nixon. *Worship: A Symphony for the Senses,* vol. 1. Macon, Ga.: Smyth and Helwys Publishing, 1998.

Multisensory resources for worship. Volume 2 contains worship services and additional resources. Very beneficial for free-church traditions.

Hickman, Hoyt L., et al., eds. *New Handbook of the Christian Year.* Nashville: Abingdon, 1992.

Planning resource with detailed explanations of seasons and individual services with historical overview and practical suggestions. Services based on the Revised Common Lectionary and The United Methodist Book of Worship. Especially useful for Holy Week.

Hymnals and Song Sources

African American Heritage Hymnal. Chicago: GIA Publications, 2001.

Classic hymns and spirituals, gospel songs, and contemporary praise songs. Extensive selection of responsive readings arranged by topic. Ecumenical.

Chalice Hymnal. St. Louis: Chalice Press, 1995.

Good range of hymns, including many texts by women and a fine selection of hymns on ecology and care of the earth. Includes prayers and brief meditations, and psalms with sung antiphons.

Evangelical Lutheran Worship. Minneapolis: Augsburg Fortress, 2006.

An outstanding new denominational hymnal with classical hymns and contemporary and global songs. Multiple musical settings for communion as well as liturgies for baptismal services, Holy Week, and morning and evening prayer.

Gather Comprehensive. Chicago: GIA Publications, 2004.

Hymnal from the Roman Catholic tradition. Engages both classical and folk genres. Accessible melodies and texts.

Global Praise. New York: General Board of Global Ministries, United Methodist Church, GBGMusik, 1997.

In three volumes. Congregational songs from around the world in the original languages (phonetic) and English.

Hymns of Glory, Songs of Praise. Norwich, U.K.: Canterbury Press, 2008.

An ecumenical and global collection of hymns and songs, including an expansive section of musical psalm settings. Extensive and helpful indexes.

Sing! A New Creation. Grand Rapids: Calvin Institute for Christian Worship, 2001.

A wonderful selection of simple hymns and songs organized both by occasions (baptism, Lord's Supper) and by movements of worship (gathering, confession and assurance, and so forth).

Sing the Journey. Scottdale, Pa.: Faith & Life Resources, 2005.

A collection of hymns and songs from a variety of traditions. Includes a good selection of global songs and shorter pieces with four-part harmonies.

Songs and Prayers from Taizé. Chicago: GIA Publications, 1991.

Christe Lux Munde: Music from Taizé. Chicago: GIA Publications, 2007.

Meditative songs, simple choruses, and chants based on traditional Christian texts from the Community of Taizé.

The Hymnal 1982: According to the Use of the Episcopal Church. New York: Church Hymnal Corporation, 1985.

Rich selection of classic hymns for every season and occasion of the Christian year.

The New Century Hymnal. Cleveland: Pilgrim Press, 1995.

A broad collection of hymns used by the United Church of Christ. Uses inclusive language and offers a good selection of texts by women hymn-writers.

The United Methodist Hymnal: Book of United Methodist Worship. Nashville: United Methodist Publishing House, 1989.

Very useful and wide-ranging hymnal that includes a liturgical psalter and numerous prayers and canticles, in addition to its comprehensive collection of hymns and congregational songs.

Eslinger, Elise, ed. *Upper Room Worshipbook: Music and Liturgies for Spiritual Formation.* Nashville: Upper Room Books, 2006.

Particularly useful in retreats or small gatherings. Multiple resources for morning and evening prayers and for singing the psalms.

Harling, Per, ed. *Worshipping Ecumenically.* Geneva, Switzerland: WCC Publications, 1995.

A broad selection of ecumenical liturgies and songs from around the world with suggestions for their appropriation.

Hickman, Hoyt L., ed. *The Psalter: Psalms and Canticles for Singing.* Louisville: Westminster John Knox, 1993.
A wide and rich variety of musical settings for all the biblical psalms and canticles with reproducible congregational responses. Accessible for congregations of every size.

Hickman, Hoyt L., ed. *The Faith We Sing.* Nashville: Abingdon, 2000.
A supplement to the United Methodist Hymnal with new hymns, songs, choruses, and service music. Comes in several editions for congregations and worship leaders. Also published with very similar content by Westminster John Knox as *Singing Our Faith*.

Saliers, Don, ed. *Sounding Glory: Hymns for the Church Year.* Portland, Ore.: OCP Publications, 2006.
A collection of unusual hymn texts (many new), set to tunes that are easy to sing, for each season of the liturgical year. Offers a brief history of texts and tunes and suggests how they might be used within a worship service.

Prayers and Liturgies

The Book of Common Prayer and Administration of the Sacraments and Other Rites and Ceremonies of the Church: Together With the Psalter or Psalms of David According to the Use of the Episcopal Church. New York: Church Hymnal Corporation, 1979.
All-inclusive prayer book easily adapted for ecumenical use.

Book of Common Worship. Louisville: Westminster John Knox, 1993.
Presbyterian resource that offers an extensive selection of prayers, rites, and orders of service. Organized by occasion.

Prayer for Each Day: Taizé. Chicago: GIA Publications, 1998.
Simple orders of worship, and prayers for contemplative Taizé-style services. Can be used together with Taizé music or as a resource for other services. Organized around the Christian year.

The Psalter. Chicago: Liturgy Training Publications, 1995.
"A faithful and inclusive rendering from the Hebrew into contemporary English poetry, intended primarily for communal song and recitation; offered for study and for comment by the International Commission on English in the Liturgy" (from the preface).

The United Methodist Book of Worship. Nashville: United Methodist Publishing House, 1992.

Official guidelines for planning worship in the United Methodist tradition, from regular Sunday services to occasional prayers and services. Draws on both traditional Wesleyan practices and ecumenical resources.

The Worship Sourcebook. Grand Rapids: Faith Alive Christian Resources, Baker Books, Calvin Institute of Christian Worship, 2004.

Comprehensive, ecumenical and reformed collection of prayers and liturgical resources, including materials for contemporary worship and worship with children. Includes CD for inserting any item in worship bulletins or projecting on screens.

Cartwright, Colbert S., and O. I. Cricket Harrison, eds. *Chalice Worship*. St. Louis: Chalice Press, 1997.

Disciples of Christ. Contains fresh, beautifully crafted services and prayers for general use and special occasions.

O'Donnell, Michael J., OSL. *Lift Up Your Hearts: Revised and Expanded, Year A*. Akron, Ohio: OSL Publications, 1995.

———. *Lift Up Your Hearts: Revised and Expanded, Year B*. Akron, Ohio: OSL Publications, 1993.

———. *Lift Up Your Hearts: Revised and Expanded, Year C*. Akron, Ohio: OSL Publications, 1989.

A collection of eucharistic prayers for every Sunday based on themes and images from the Revised Common Lectionary.

Scagnelli, Peter J. *Prayers for Sundays and Seasons, Year A*. Chicago: Liturgy Training Publications, 1998.

———. *Prayers for Sundays and Seasons, Year B*. Chicago: Liturgy Training Publications, 1996.

———. *Prayers for Sundays and Seasons, Year C*. Chicago: Liturgy Training Publications, 1997.

Helpful worship planning resources based on both the Roman Catholic and Revised Common Lectionaries. Includes a good selection of intercessory petitions.

Tirabassi, Maren C., and Kathy Wonson Eddy. *Gifts of Many Cultures: Worship Resources for the Global Community*. Cleveland: Pilgrim Press, 1995.

Prayers, complete worship services, graphics, and poetry from around the world.

Visual Arts and Multisensory Worship

Chinn, Nancy. *Spaces for Spirit: Adorning the Church.* Chicago: Liturgy Training Publications, 1989.

Clear evidence, through beautifully written text and exquisite color plates, of the power of visual arts and artists in the church.

Lawrence, Kenneth T. *Imaging the Word: An Arts and Lectionary Resource,* vol. 1. Cleveland: United Church Press, 1994.

Blain, Susan A. *Imaging the Word: An Arts and Lectionary Resource,* vol. 2. Cleveland: United Church Press, 1995.

———. *Imaging the Word: An Arts and Lectionary Resource,* vol. 3. Cleveland: United Church Press, 1996.

These three volumes (roughly organized by lectionary year) provide prayers, texts, and rich artwork to be used for bulletins, visual designs, meditations, and multimedia presentations. Virtually required for anyone serious about introducing multisensory engagement in worship, as well as connecting church and culture.

Mazar, Peter. *To Crown the Year: Decorating the Church through the Seasons.* Chicago: Liturgy Training Publications, 1995.

Helpful and practical suggestions for visual designs, especially using natural materials, with attention to the liturgical year.

Sudbrock, Eleanore Feucht. *Seasons for Praise: Art for the Sanctuary.* St. Louis: Concordia, 2000.

Illustrated collection of ideas for visual design. Includes patterns and pictures for temporary and permanent, easy and complex liturgical artwork and banners.

Online Resources

Calvin Institute for Christian Worship. http://www.calvin.edu/worship.

Rich array of resources, very helpful suggestions and articles, links to other sites, training events and symposiums, book reviews. An all-encompassing and easily accessed site.

Planning Center. http://www.planningcenteronline.com
Resource and planning tool that lets you look for music, link to audio tracks, develop flow charts for musicians and liturgists, send e-mail reminders.

Jan Richardson Images. http//www.janrichardsonimages.com
The website of gifted contemporary artist Jan Richardson. Very affordable subscription for full use of images.

The Revised Common Lectionary. http://lectionary.library.vanderbilt.edu/
An excellent resource for weekly lectionary readings, prayers, and artwork.

The Text This Week. http://www.textweek.com
The place to begin. Lectionary-based planning resources and articles, art, music, movies, devotionals, with links to specific denominational sites.

Worship. http://www.gbod.org/worship/
Worship site of the United Methodist Board of Discipleship. Fine lectionary resources for both traditional and contemporary worship planning and preaching, with good links to other helpful sites.

Organizations

Denominational and ecumenical associations with a wide range of resources and sponsored events

Association of Anglican Musicians. http://www.anglicanmusicians.org/

Association of Lutheran Church Musicians. http://www.alcm.org/

Choristers Guild. http://www.choristersguild.org/

Fellowship of United Methodists in Music and Worship Arts. http://www.umfellowship.org

Presbyterian Association of Musicians. http://www.presbymusic.org/

National Association of Pastoral Musicians. (Roman Catholic) http://www.npm.org/